P9-EAY-827

THE MEDICI AESOP

THE MEDICI AESOP

Spencer MS 50

From the Spencer Collection of
The New York Public Library

Introduction by Everett Fahy

Fables Translated from the Greek
by Bernard McTigue

Harry N. Abrams, Inc., Publishers, New York

Editor: Adele Westbrook
Designer: Carol Robson
Photo Editor: John K. Crowley

Photography by Philip Pocock

LIBRARY OF CONGRESS CATALOGING-IN-PUBLICATION DATA

Aesop's fables. English & Greek.
    The Medici Aesop: Spencer MS 50 from the Spencer Collection
of The New York Public Library/introduction by Everett Fahy;
fables translated from the Greek by Bernard McTigue.
        p.   cm.
    Bibliography: p. 169
    Includes index.
    ISBN 0-8109-1542-1
        1. Fables, Greek—Translations into English. 2. Fables, English—
Translations from Greek. 3. Medici Aesop. 4. Illumination of
books and manuscripts, Italian—Italy—Florence. 5. Illumination of
books and manuscripts, Renaissance—Italy—Florence.
6. Manuscripts, Greek—Italy—Florence. 7. Medici, Piero de',
1416–1469—Library. I. Aesop. II. McTigue, Bernard. III. Title.
PA3855.E5M33 1989
398.2'452—dc19   89-96

Text copyright © 1989 Harry N. Abrams, Inc.

Illustrations copyright © 1989 The New York Public Library

Published in 1989 by Harry N. Abrams, Incorporated, New York
All rights reserved. No part of the contents of this book may be
reproduced without the written permission of the publisher

A Times Mirror Company

Printed and bound in Japan

CONTENTS

INTRODUCTION

The copy of Aesop's fables in the Spencer Collection of The New York Public Library (Spencer MS 50) holds a special place in the history of art. With its limpid illustrations and its handwritten Greek text, this small, compact volume (easily held in one hand), typifies the elegant sensibility of Florentine humanism at the end of the fifteenth century.

Aesop's fables are brief accounts of incidents or conversations wherein animals often speak and act like human beings, or where people contend with one another, or in which either animals or people confront the gods. The characters usually have a single trait, and the story often turns on a single act intended to teach a lesson in morality or worldliness. Jean de La Fontaine put it succinctly in the introduction to his *Fables choisies* of 1668–94: "A fable consists of two parts which might be termed body and soul; the story being the body and the moral the soul."

Over the centuries, Aesop's fables have never lost their appeal. Which child does not know "The Fox and the Grapes," or "The Tortoise and the Hare"? The first version in English, *The Book of Subtle Histories and Fables of Aesop*, was produced by William Caxton (c. 1421–91), who learned printing at the age of fifty in Cologne. He set up a press in London, near Westminster Abbey, and published his *Aesop* on March 26, 1484. Countless writers have added to the rich store of fables, from La Fontaine and John Dryden in the seventeenth century to James Thurber and George Orwell in our own time.

By the fifth century B.C., fables had become a popular form of literature, and the Greeks credited Aesop as their author. Supposedly a deformed Phrygian slave, Aesop is said to have lived from about 620 to 560 B.C. Since there is no reliable information concerning his life, some writers claim that he never existed. They argue that the telling of fables is a custom dating back to primeval times when man lived in close contact with both tame animals and wild beasts.

The earliest authority for the existence of Aesop is the historian Herodotus, who lived in the fifth century B.C. He speaks of Aesop as a well-known author of fables who was murdered a hundred years earlier by the inhabitants of Delphi. Later writers have embellished this account: Aristophanes, the comic playwright who died in the early fourth century B.C., says that the Delphians accused Aesop of stealing a silver cup from their temple; Plutarch (A.D. 46?–c. 120) says the Delphians killed Aesop by hurling him from a precipice.

Assuming there really was a man called Aesop who invented fables, we can be certain that he did not write them down. Memorized and recited,

Aesopic fables were part of an oral tradition within which successive storytellers took many liberties and recast the fables to suit themselves and their circumstances. After Aesop's supposed lifetime, any fable that resembled his type of tale was attributed to him. Paradoxically, there are even some fables that predate their alleged author. A startling example occurs in Aristophanes's *The Birds* (c. 300 B.C.), where the fable of "The Eagle and the Vixen," which was already known in the eighth century B.C., is called a fable of Aesop. Several animal stories that read almost word for word like Aesop's fables have been found on Egyptian papyri dating from about 1600 B.C.

While in prison, Socrates (469–399 B.C.) reputedly began to cast Aesop's fables into verse, but nothing seems to have come of this work. The first recorded collection of Aesop's fables was compiled about 300 B.C. by Demetrius of Phalerum, a governor of Athens who later became a librarian at Alexandria. All we know about his collection is that it was written in ten books, which have not survived. The earliest extant collection is a retelling of the stories in Latin verse by Phaedrus, a Greek slave who became a freedman under Augustus, and who composed his verses during the reign of Tiberius (A.D. 14–37). Another collection, made by Babrius, a Roman living in Syria during the early third century, was not discovered until 1844 in a monastery on Mount Athos. A certain Avianus translated forty-two of the fables into Latin elegiacs about A.D. 400. In later centuries, the verses of Phaedrus and Avianus, together with some anonymous collections in Greek prose, served writers who added fables from other sources–and probably included some of their own invention. The most valuable collection was made by Maximum Planudes, a learned Byzantine monk who died at

the age of fifty about the year 1310. Planudes's text is the basis for almost all the subsequent versions of Aesop's fables that have proliferated in European literature during the past six hundred years.

By the Middle Ages, Aesop was the subject of a biography, most probably written by Planudes, that enjoyed almost as much fame as the fables. This fanciful life portrays Aesop as a humpbacked bondsman whose ugliness made people laugh. But his talent for narrating fables enabled him to outwit his masters. Thus, he won his freedom, became an adviser to kings, and had many adventures. The Spencer manuscript probably began with this biography. The manuscript obviously has lost some leaves; and since its signature numbers start at VI, about forty-five percent of the manuscript must be missing, which is about the length of the life of Aesop in similar manuscripts that include both the biography and the fables.

The Spencer Aesop differs from other versions of the fables in that it was copied from a printed book, namely, the first Greek edition of Planudes's life of Aesop and 144 fables. This *editio princeps* was published about 1480 in Milan by Bono Accurzio, together with a Latin translation by Rinuccio Aretino. As Jeffrey Kaimowitz and Bernard McTigue have observed, the scribe who copied the text of Accurzio's edition knew his Greek well enough to correct some spelling, yet he also made errors of his own, and carelessly omitted several words. But the important point is that the original owner of the Spencer Aesop, or a generous friend of that first owner, commissioned a costly handwritten version of a book that was available in a printed version at the time.

This shows that the invention of printing did not abruptly end the age of the illuminated manuscript. Early printed books–or incunabula, as books published before 1500 are called–coexisted for several decades with newly-made manuscripts, much as motor vehicles and horsedrawn carriages mingled in our city streets at the turn of the twentieth century. The earliest printed books were produced in the Rhineland soon after 1450 and spread to Italy only in the summer of 1465, when two Germans, Conrad Schweynheym and Arnold Pannartz, set up a press in the Benedictine monastery of Santa Scolastica at Subiaco, not far from Rome. Eleven years later, some Benedictine nuns established a printing house in their abbey at Ripoli, several miles southeast of Florence.

This revolutionary technique immediately made it possible to produce virtually unlimited copies of texts with a speed and economy that many contemporaries found inconceivable. Yet scribes still pursued their slow and silent task of lettering parchment codices, particularly when the text was needed in fewer copies than a printer found it economical to reproduce. Scribes also were kept busy by humanist bibliophiles who simply would not tolerate printed books in their libraries. The Florentine book agent, Vespasiano da Bisticci, writing about 1482, states that the Duke of Urbino wished "to create the finest library since antiquity. . . . In his library all the books are superlative, and written with the pen, and had there been one printed volume it would have been ashamed in such company."

But printed books found a ready market. Of Aesop's fables, approximately 150 different editions–in English, French, German, Italian, Latin, and Greek–had been published before 1500, many of them illustrated with woodcuts. The earliest one was Ulrich Boner's *Der Edelstein* (Bamberg, 1461), which also enjoys the distinction of being the first dated illustrated book to be printed. Leo-

nardo da Vinci seems to have had no qualms about owning printed books. While working on his ill-fated fresco of *The Battle of Anghiari* (1504), he stored 116 books in two chests at the hospital of Santa Maria Novella in Florence. From the invaluable list he drew up for his records, we know that three of them were editions of Aesop's fables: two published in Italy and one, *Les Fables de Esope*, at Lyons. Leonardo's interest in Aesop is confirmed by the twenty fables he composed in his notebooks. (In this regard, he once again followed in the footsteps of his great predecessor, Leon Battista Alberti, who wrote 100 fables in the Aesopian vein. They were published posthumously in the first Italian edition of Alberti's treatise *Della pittura*.)

In Florence, on the ides of January 1488–about the time the Spencer Aesop was created–Bernardo Nerli published the first printed edition in Greek of Homer's works. A deluxe copy of this book in the National Library in Naples is printed on parchment rather than paper, and it is exquisitely decorated to make it resemble an illuminated manuscript. It contains a letter in Latin dedicating the work to Lorenzo the Magnificent's son, Piero de' Medici, then aged eighteen. Its illuminations and an almost life-size portrait of Piero were painted by Gherardo di Giovanni, the greatest of all late fifteenth-century Florentine miniaturists, about whom more will be said below.

The study of Greek was an innovation of the Renaissance. Throughout the Middle Ages, Latin had been the language of the clergy and the small elite class of educated men. But with the rise of humanism and a new interest in classical studies, learned men became dissatisfied with corrupt texts of the work of the ancient Greeks. This led to an intense search for accurate texts and for copies of missing works. Only by rediscovering lost works and by correcting known ones could Renaissance humanists hope to gain a valid knowledge of classical learning and antique art.

The founders of the humanist movement, Francesco Petrarch (1304–74) and Giovanni Boccaccio (1313–75), were so frustrated by medieval Latin translations of Greek classics that they struggled to learn Greek on their own. But the language barrier was not broken effectively until 1397, when a Greek scholar from Constantinople, Emanuel Chrysoloras, began to teach in Florence. One of his students, Poggio Bracciolini (1380–1459), ransacked old monasteries in Northern Europe searching for ancient texts to send back to Florence. From London, on March 5, 1420, he wrote: "I want to drink in the Greek greedily so as to escape those horrid translations, which so torment me that I feel more irritation in the style than pleasure in the matter." Later, Cosimo de' Medici summoned Giovanni Argyropoulos to teach Greek in Florence for fifteen years, and among his pupils were Poliziano, Lorenzo de' Medici, and John, Duke of Gloucester. Poliziano (1454–94), who became one of the tutors of Lorenzo de' Medici's children, introduced his lectures on Homer with the boast that "the Attic tongue, torn from its own soil by barbarians, now echoes in the mouths of youths of the most noble families in Florence." There is a high degree of probability that the Spencer Aesop was made for one of these youths. With its engaging illustrations and appealing fables, it would have been a seductive way to teach Greek to a schoolboy.

There is no documentary evidence concerning the identity of the scribe who copied the Greek text or the artist who illuminated the Spencer Aesop. But there is overwhelming visual evidence that the artist was Gherardo di Giovanni (1444–97). He belonged to the same generation as Botticelli (c. 1445–1510), Ghirlandaio (1449–94), and Leonardo da Vinci (1452–1519). In the sixteenth century, his fame was so great that Vasari devoted an entire chapter to him in *Le vite de' più eccellenti pittori, scultori ed architettori* (1550), whereas today he is little known beyond a small circle of art historians.

As a boy, Gherardo studied literature with Poliziano. How the son of a stonemason was accorded this opportunity is unknown. Five letters to his fellow pupil, Barolomeo Dei (a Florentine official not to be confused with the artist, Bartolomeo della Gatta), survive from the 1480s. Gherardo composed them in Latin and proudly signed them *Gerardus Apelleius*, alluding to Apelles, the celebrated ancient Greek painter. While Vasari praises the illuminations that Gherardo made for Florentine churches and for such discriminating bibliophiles as Filippo Strozzi, Francesco Sassetti, King Matthias Corvinus of Hungary, and Dom Manuel, the future King of Portugal, he emphasizes Gherardo's versatility in the arts. Unlike professional miniaturists who worked exclusively on a small scale, Gherardo frescoed roadside tabernacles, painted murals on the façades of churches, and produced large altarpieces. He also was an accomplished musician; for playing the organ in the Florentine church of Sant' Egidio, he received regular payments from 1470 to 1494. According to Vasari, he even made etchings in the manner of Schongauer and Dürer, but none of these has been identified.

His panel paintings were recognized only fairly recently. Since they were not signed, Gherardo's connection with them had been forgotten over the intervening centuries. But modern scholars assembled a group of religious paintings and a set of secular panels by an anonymous master named after an enchantingly beautiful picture entitled *The Triumph of Chastity* in the Galleria Sabauda in Turin. In 1967 these paintings by the Master of *The Triumph of Chastity* were convincingly identified as Gherardo's.

Because of Gherardo's ingenuity, he became involved in a project to decorate the interior of the Cathedral of Florence with mosaics. Knowing that frescoes fade with time, Lorenzo de' Medici decided to emulate the ancients and revive the lost art of glass mosaic. He encouraged the wardens of the Cathedral to commission Botticelli, Ghirlandaio, and Gherardo to cover the vault of the chapel of Saint Zenobius with mosaics. Their work came to a halt soon after Lorenzo's death in 1492—today only ornamental bands of mosaic on the ribs of the vault remain.

Time and weather have not been kind to Gherardo's frescoes. The large scene he painted in 1474 on the façade of the hospital of Santa Maria Nuova suffered so much from its exposed position that, in the sixteenth century, drastic repairs were already necessary. A tabernacle he frescoed in 1487 was pulled down in the nineteenth century to make way for the present-day Piazza Beccaria (a small fragment of the fresco survives on a wall nearby). Ignored today by the throngs of tourists making their way to the Fra Angelico Museum is another fresco that Gherardo painted in 1482 in a tabernacle attached to a house at the corner of the Piazza San Marco and Via Cavour. Known as the *Madonna della rosa*, it is a lovely work depicting the Madonna and Child with two angels holding lilies, flanked on the side walls by six male saints.

The house on the corner of the Piazza San Marco belonged to Gherardo's father, Giovanni di Miniato (c. 1398–1479/80), sometimes called Del Fora–a nickname his sons never used, although later writers have often assigned it to them. As a stonemason, Giovanni di Miniato worked for Donatello and Michelozzo, among others, and he owned several houses in the city, as well as a small farm not far away. He had four sons: by his first wife there was Miniato (born 1439/40), who became a monk; and by his second wife there was Bartolomeo di Giovanni (1444–after 1501), Gherardo di Giovanni, and Monte di Giovanni (1448–1532/33).

The youngest three became artists. The eldest of these, Bartolomeo, was a prolific painter of Madonnas and panels illustrating Greek and Roman legends. Like Gherardo's large-scale paintings, Bartolomeo's works were rediscovered in the twentieth century. Over sixty of them were assigned to an anonymous follower, or "*alunno*," of Domenico Ghirlandaio by Bernard Berenson in the first issue of *The Burlington Magazine* (1903). Since one of the paintings Berenson attributed to his "Alunno di Domenico" was the predella of Ghirlandaio's Innocenti altarpiece, for which Bartolomeo di Giovanni was paid seventeen florins in 1488, here was proof that the "Alunno di Domenico" was Bartolomeo di Giovanni. The distinction between the types of painting done by Bartolomeo and Gherardo was noted on February 2, 1472 in a ledger of the Company of Saint Luke, a religious society to which many Florentine painters belonged. Bartolomeo is listed as a "*sargjaio*," a painter of processional banners, whereas Gherardo is called a "*miniatore*." (The long-lived youngest son, Monte di Giovanni–who specialized in manuscript illumination–often collaborated with Gherardo, and imitated his style long after Gherardo's death.)

In October 1460, as a boy of fifteen or sixteen, Gherardo executed his earliest recorded illuminations—for Bartolomeo Scala, an influential associate of Lorenzo de' Medici. Four years later, Gherardo went into business with his brothers. Together, Gherardo, Bartolomeo, and Monte rented a workshop from the monks of the Badia and set up a stationer's shop, a few steps away from the famous above-mentioned bookseller, Vespasiano da Bisticci, who employed dozens of copyists and illuminators to produce volumes for the libraries of the Medici, the Duke of Urbino, and Pope Nicholas V. Bartolomeo di Giovanni acted as the manager, while Gherardo and Monte sold paper and parchment, bound new and old books, and illuminated antiphonals for local churches, as well as manuscripts for private individuals. The partnership broke up in 1475 when the two younger brothers discovered that Bartolomeo had been selling things without sharing the proceeds with them. Their elderly father resolved the dispute—Bartolomeo withdrew from the business and, curiously enough, remained on good terms with his brothers. Gherardo, who never married, continued to live with Bartolomeo and his growing family, while Monte stayed with his mother and father.

Until recently, it was virtually impossible to distinguish Gherardo di Giovanni's style from Monte's. Because they collaborated on many manuscripts (and sometimes employed assistants), their output varied. Only in 1962 did Mirella Levi d'Ancona identify an illumination in a breviary now in the Bargello in Florence, a part of which Gherardo had painted on his own in 1477 for the hospital of Santa Maria Nuova. Since then, several other books have been recognized as works illuminated by Gherardo—without the collabora-

tion of Monte—among them, a copy of Livy's *The Second Punic War* commissioned in 1479 by King Ferdinand II of Aragon and now in the university library at Valencia, a psalter bearing the Medici arms and now in the Fitzwilliam Museum at Cambridge, and a copy of Statius's *Achilleis* (also bearing the Medici arms), now in the Biblioteca Riccardiana in Florence. All are notable for their extraordinarily high quality.

In contrast to Monte's rather confusingly crowded compositions, Gherardo's miniatures are lucidly structured. Each figure is a thoughtfully observed individual, not a stereotype. Gherardo's handling of paint is distinctive, too. There is nothing mechanical about the way his brush moved. Figures and objects in the foreground are clear, those farther away recede into the misty distance. His subtle rendering of optical effects caught the eye of Leonardo da Vinci, who made a note on one of his drawings now at Windsor Castle to remind himself to save for the last chapter of his Book on Light and Shade a discussion of the figures he had seen in Gherardo's scriptorium.

The wonder of Gherardo's success in rendering light and atmosphere is that he did it by employing the conventional techniques that miniaturists had used for centuries. First, he applied gold leaf to the parchment, laying it down on glue and then burnishing it until it shone. He ground his pigments by hand and mixed them with glair, which is made by beating egg white to a froth and then allowing it to stand until it becomes a watery liquid. To vary the intensity of his colors, Gherardo's only option was to dilute the mixture with water.

In the Spencer Aesop there is a happy balance between the imagined pictorial space of the illustrations and the flat surface of the page. Gherardo achieved this by neatly isolating the illustrations within gold frames. The script, the squared-off initials, and the decorative borders lie on the surface. The borders consist of stylized flowers, green leaves, dots of gold leaf, and a filigree in pen and ink that gives a charming lightness to the columns of script.

The first folio differs from the rest. Here, a scroll of gold foliage decorates a blue band on the left and a red band at the bottom. At the top, two seated harts flank a central medallion of trompe-l'oeil pearls and gold-flecked blue stones. At the ends of the top border are two smaller medallions of pearls surrounding cut rubies. These motifs recall the work of Girolamo da Cremona, a Northern Italian miniaturist whose daring illusionism made a lasting impression upon Gherardo. The jeweled medallions and the pair of seated harts also appear on Girolamo's splendid frontispiece for the 1483 printed edition of Aristotle's works in the Pierpont Morgan Library. Gherardo gained firsthand knowledge of Girolamo's style when they collaborated between 1473 and 1477 on the decoration of the above-mentioned breviary for the hospital of Santa Maria Nuova.

A roundel in the border at the bottom of folio 1 in the Spencer Aesop shows a half-length portrait of Aesop as a well-fed figure standing before a landscape and dressed like a Florentine of the late fifteenth century in a red tunic highlighted with touches of gold. Gherardo di Giovanni painted a similar portrait roundel in a sumptuously decorated copy of the 1476 printed edition of Pliny's *Natural History*, now in the Bodleian Library at Oxford; it depicts Filippo Strozzi, who commissioned Gherardo to furnish the illuminations. The roundels are much the same, except that Strozzi's portrait is not of an imaginary figure, and the Duomo of Florence can be seen over his shoulder.

Since Aesop's fables are not fixed in time or place, artists who have illustrated them have tended to use familiar settings. Gherardo di Giovanni was no exception. Although the illuminations in the Spencer Aesop do not include topographical views of Florence, the architecture is thoroughly Florentine and the scenes are populated with figures dressed in the style of late fifteenth-century Florence. In "The Old Woman and the Doctor" (folios 13v–14v), for example, the doctor wears a typical Florentine red robe with a scarlet *becchetto*, a peculiarly Florentine headdress. In "The Thieves and the Rooster" (folios 51v–52r), the thieves are three Florentine youths outfitted with doublets and hose. On the far right, a Florentine citizen awakens in a Quattrocento bed mounted with a wooden headboard and set on a raised platform. He pulls a white undershirt over his head and, once on his feet, dons a blue doublet.

Gherardo also shows us Florentine ateliers. In "Hermes and the Sculptor" (folios 47v–48r), he depicts two portrait busts on a shelf and two marble putti on the floor, in addition to the statues mentioned in the fable. A portrait bust casts a shadow on the wall in "The Fox and the Mask" (folios 8r–8v). Behind the fox is a typical Florentine marble relief of the Madonna in a blue-and-gold frame. On the wall, a lifelike portrait of a young man recalls the charming self-portrait that Gherardo shows himself painting in the Bodleian copy of Pliny's *Natural History* mentioned above.

Another tie with fifteenth-century Florence is the inclusion of the Medici arms in the illumination of "The Dog Who Came to Dinner" (folios 68r–69r): a gold shield with six blue balls is visible on the wall beneath the cupboard. One might take this as evidence that the manuscript was made for a Medici, like the Homer in the National Library,

Naples, that was presented to the young Piero de' Medici. However, it is also true that the Medici arms appear frequently in works of art commissioned by various wealthy Florentine families—especially those loyal to Lorenzo de' Medici. They are found, for example, in a Book of Hours in the Bibliothèque Nationale, Paris, that was a wedding present for Jacopo de' Nerli and Lisabetta Sassetti. And, in one of Bartolomeo di Giovanni's finest works, a panel in the Prado illustrating *The Feast in the Pine Forest*, the shields of the Pucci, Bini, and Medici families all appear. As the picture was painted to celebrate the marriage in 1483 of Giannozzo Pucci to the second of his three wives, Lucrezia Bini, the arms of the Medici serve only to compliment the leader of the Florentine Republic. Giannozzo Pucci was so steadfast to the Medici that he was beheaded in 1497 for his part in a conspiracy to reestablish Piero de' Medici's control of Florence. Similarly, two red pennants bearing the Medici arms appear in one of the panels painted in 1487 to celebrate the marriage of Lorenzo Tornabuoni and Giovanna degli Albizzi. Lorenzo Tornabuoni was named after his uncle, Lorenzo de' Medici, and—like Giannozzo Pucci—he also was decapitated in 1497 for his continued support of the Medici.

Until someone discovers the frontispiece of the Spencer Aesop, we cannot be absolutely sure for whom it was made. But we do know that Piero de' Medici owned an illuminated manuscript of Aesop's fables with a Greek text. It is listed as "*Fabule Esopi, in menbranis, historiate, grece*" in the inventory that was made of Piero's library in October 1495, shortly after he was expelled from Florence. Since we know of no other illuminated, late fifteenth-century Florentine copy of Aesop in Greek, this inventory record points to Piero de'

Medici as the likely possessor of the Spencer Aesop. By virtue of his knowledge of Greek, Piero is also the most plausible person to have owned this manuscript. From the age of three, he was tutored by Poliziano. When he was seven, he wrote a letter in Latin to his father in which he reported that, "I have already learned many verses of Virgil and I know almost the whole first book of Theodorus by heart, and understand it too, I think." Piero's sisters and his younger brothers, Giovanni (1475–1521), the future Pope Leo X, and Giuliano (1479–1516), later Duke of Nemours, had ecclesiastical tutors and are not known to have read Greek.

As the eldest son of Lorenzo de' Medici, Piero was the heir apparent, but his fate was not an enviable one. A few days after Lorenzo's death on April 8, 1492, the government councils of Florence elected Piero to all the offices formerly held by his father. Thus, at the age of twenty-one, he became the unofficial dictator of the merchant oligarchy that had ruled Florence for nearly sixty years. Unfortunately, he soon proved himself incapable of dealing with the crisis caused by the invasion of Italy by Charles VIII of France. In November 1494, when the Florentines learned that Piero had secretly agreed to allow the French army to pass through their city, they banished him from Tuscany and a mob was permitted to plunder his palace. He fled with his family to Bologna and then to Venice. Three years later, in an effort to reinstate himself, he made a half-hearted attempt to enter Florence with troops borrowed from the Venetian Republic. His ill-fated adherents opened the city gates, but he retreated. Ultimately, he allied himself with the French and was drowned in December 1503 after a battle near Naples between French and Spanish troops. He had saved four cannons from capture by the Spaniards, but their weight caused his boat to capsize. Thus, his nickname–"Piero the Unfortunate"–seems to have been well deserved.

In the nineteenth century, the Spencer Aesop belonged to the Reverend Henry Joseph Thomas Drury (1778–1841). It is next recorded in the library of Sir Thomas Phillipps (1792–1872). His enormous collection of rare books was dispersed in a series of sixteen sales between 1888 and 1949. The Aesop came up for auction in London on July 1, 1946 as part of the "Bibliotheca Phillippica : A Further Portion of the Renowned Library Formed by the late Sir Thomas Phillipps." The manuscript was purchased by The New York Public Library with funds from the bequest of William Augustus Spencer, a collector primarily of illustrated French books dating from about 1800 to 1910. He went down with the *Titanic* in April 1912, but his bequest has enabled the Library to acquire since then nearly 10,000 rare books and European and Asian manuscripts.

The present publication of MS 50 from the Spencer Collection, under the title of *The Medici Aesop*, will make it possible for this superb volume to be appreciated and enjoyed by a much wider audience than those fortunate few who have had the pleasure of studying the original in the Print Room of The New York Public Library.[1]

1. *Since the illustrations or "miniatures" in the manuscript precede the relevant Greek text, the fable pictured may not always be written on the same folio as the illustration, or only a portion of the fable text may appear on the same folio. The English-language translation of each fable (which has been placed as close to the illustration of that fable as possible) includes a notation after the title of the fable that identifies the folios upon which the illustration and Greek text appear. In addition, there are fables for which the illustrations are missing and, in one instance, there is an illustration of a fable for which the text is missing. These lacunae have also been indicated in each case before the translation of the relevant fable.*

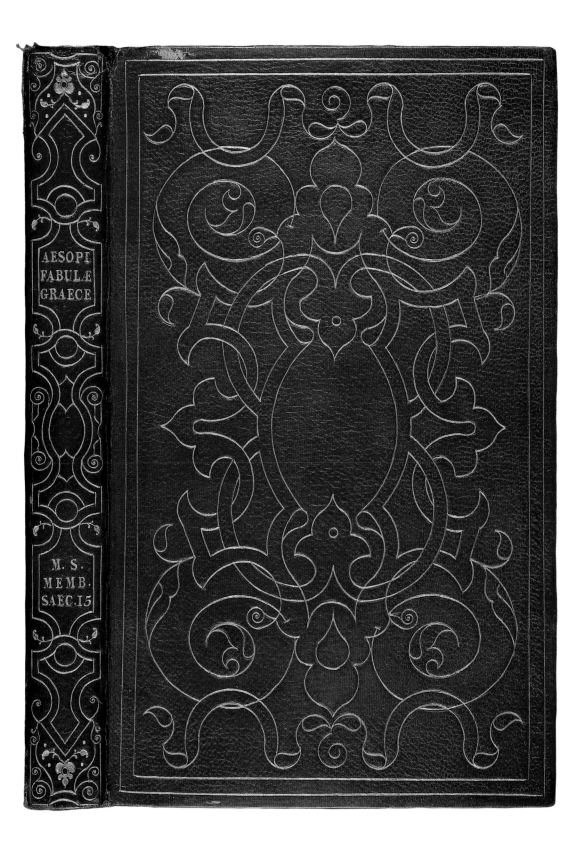

17

The Fables of Aesop in Greek a MS on Vellum of the 15th Century of great beauty and value, executed in Italy.

The Initial Letters are beautifully executed in gold and colours, with Ornaments of flowers and vases. —

The Volume contains also 131. Miniatures exquisitely painted representing the subjects of the Fables. —

Some of the Leaves, at the end, are damaged. —

Rev. Theodore Williams
Sale Cat. 1827

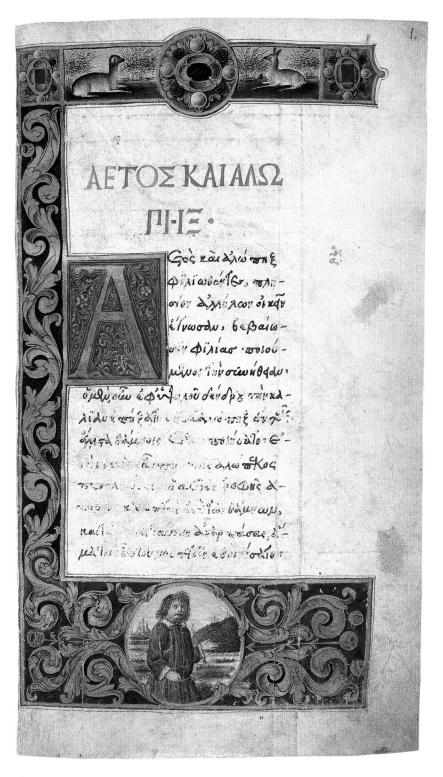

THE
MEDICI
AESOP

THE EAGLE AND THE FOX

(Folios 1r–2r)

[Greek text only. The miniature is missing.]

An eagle and a fox, having become friends, decided to build their nests close together, since they thought that this would strengthen their friendship. And so, the eagle built her nest high up in a tree and the fox made a nest for her cubs in the bushes at the tree's base. One day, while the fox was out looking for food for her family, the eagle—in need of food for *her* young ones—swooped down to the fox's nest, made off with the unprotected cubs, and fed them to her eaglets. When the fox returned and saw what had happened, she was less distressed by the death of her children than infuriated by the impossibility of avenging them. Since she could not take flight and catch the eagle, she was forced to content herself with cursing the villainous bird from afar.

But the eagle soon had to pay for her crime against friendship. One day, in a nearby field, some peasants offered up a goat to the gods on a fiery altar. The eagle, seeing this, swept down and grasped a flaming portion of the sacrifice in her talons. But when she flew back with it to her nest, she neglected to take into account the force of the wind, which fanned the flames and set the nest on fire. The eaglets, still unable to fly, tumbled from the nest to the ground, where the fox was waiting. In the twinkling of an eye, she gobbled them all up.

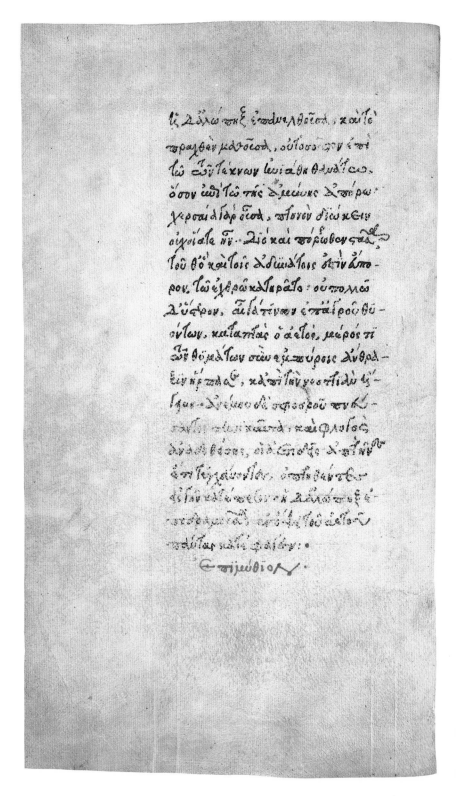

The moral of this fable is: Beware of being a false friend. You may think some weak friend you have wronged is powerless to do you any harm, but you will not escape the vengeance of heaven.

THE EAGLE AND THE BEETLE
(Folios 2r–3r)

One day, while an eagle was out hunting, she caught sight of a hare and pursued it. The hare ran as fast as she could, but soon realized that escape was impossible. In desperation, the hare sought the help of the only creature she could see nearby, which happened to be a beetle. The beetle tried to protect the hare by begging the eagle not to kill the terrified creature. But the eagle sneered at the puny little beetle and, with a look of contempt, wolfed down the hare right in front of the protesting insect.

The beetle vowed revenge. She followed the bird everywhere, and waited until the eagle built a nest and laid her eggs. Then, when the eagle left to search for food, the beetle would fly up to the nest and push the eggs out, sending them crashing to the ground.

At her wit's end, the eagle finally went to Zeus, the god of whom she is the emblem, and asked for his help. Zeus was sympathetic and allowed the eagle to lay her eggs in his lap. But the wily beetle

was not deterred by this divine inter-
cession. She rolled some dung into a
small ball, flew over Zeus, and dropped
it in his lap. Surprised and disgusted,
Zeus leapt up to shake the dung from
his clothes and, without meaning to,
allowed the eagle's eggs to crash to the
ground. Since that time, they say, eagles
don't make nests when beetles are
in season.

The moral of this fable is: Take care not
to express contempt for anyone. However
insignificant they may seem, you can be
sure that, one day, they will find a way
to repay you—with interest.

καὶ σὺν τῷ βῃ πεσοῦ τ'. μαθὼν
δὲ πρὸς τοῦ κανθάρ8. ὅτι αὐτὲ-
λιας, τοὺς ἀετοὺς ἀμεῶν ὁμῆς, οὐγὰρ
δὴ τὸν κάνθαρον ἐκεῖνος μόνον ἐ-
δίωκεν, ἀλλὰ καὶ εἰς τὸν δία αὐτὸν ἀνέβκα, πρὸς τὸν ἀετὸν εἶπεν
ἐλθοῦ7α, καὶ θάρον εἶναι τὸν λυ-
πούν7α, καὶ δ δὴ καὶ δικαίως λίπ̄
μὴ βουλόμενος ἐλ ηλθ ὐος τὸ ζῶν
ἁ ετὸν ἐσφαλίσ7αι τῆς συνηθούς δε
τῶν κανθάρω διαδαλζ προς τὸν
ἀετὸν ὅλεοι. τοῦ δε μετιστορμῆ,
ἐκεῖθ εν ἀναχωρήσαν7ος τοῦ ζῶν
ἁ ετῶν μὴ δ ὅλως γενέσθαι, μέχρα
δ ἂν μὴ φαίνων7αι κανθάρου:·

Ἐπιμυθιον·

ὁ μῦθος δηλοῖ μηδένος καταφρο-
νεῖν, λογιζομένος ὡς οὐδείς ἐ-
στι, ὃς πεπονθειῶς κακῶς οὐκ
ἂν δύναιτό τι ω̃ αυτὸν ἀπαμῦ-

THE NIGHTINGALE AND THE
SPARROW HAWK

(Folios 3v–4r)

A nightingale was perched high up in an oak tree, chirping away in her usual manner. A passing sparrow hawk saw her and, being rather hungry, swept down and grasped her in his talons. Seeing that she was about to die, the nightingale begged the sparrow hawk to let her go, saying that a poor little bird such as she could not possibly satisfy a sparrow hawk's hunger. The sparrow hawk was not convinced. "Wouldn't it be stupid of me," he replied, "to drop you, when there are no larger birds in sight?"

The moral of this fable is: A small bird in the talons is worth any number of larger ones over the horizon.

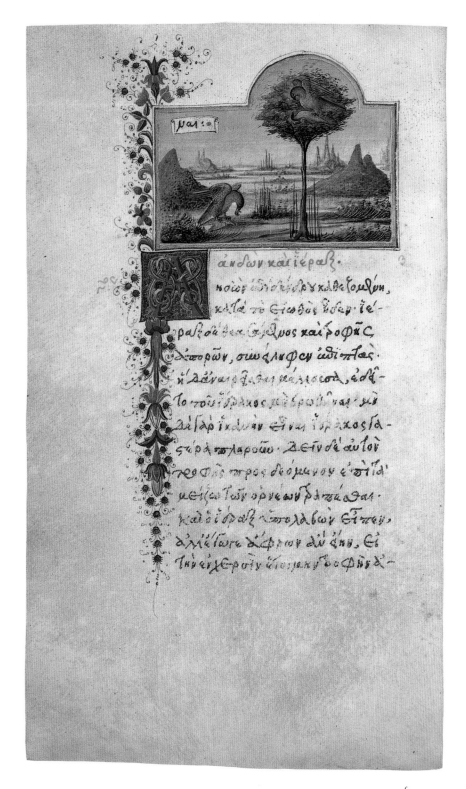

f. 3v

24

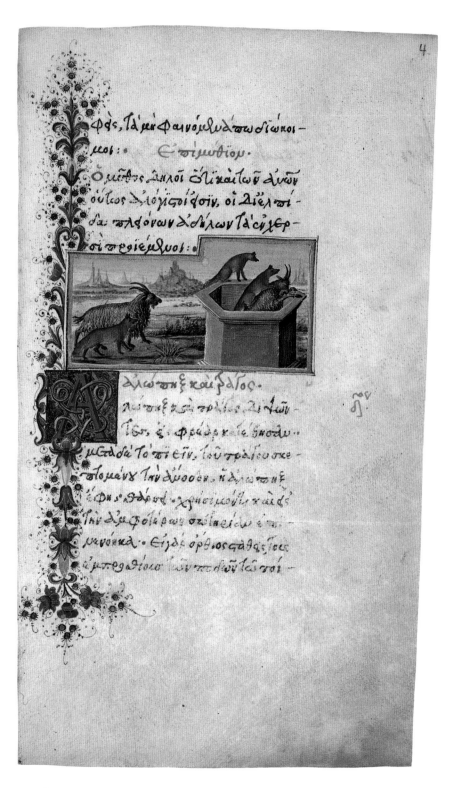

4

THE FOX AND THE GOAT

(*Folios 4r–5r*)

One day, a fox tumbled into a well and couldn't manage to climb back up. After a while, a thirsty goat wandered up to the edge of the well, and seeing the fox down below, asked him if the water was safe to drink. The fox, making the best of a bad situation, praised the quality of the water and suggested that the goat come down for a drink. The goat leaped in immediately, without thinking of anything but his thirst. When he had drunk his fill, he asked the fox how he could get back up. The fox replied: "I have a plan that will get us both out of here. Put your two front legs against the wall and hold your horns up. I will climb up your back, onto your horns, and leap out of the well. Once I'm out, I'll help you up." The goat agreed, and the fox was out of the well in a flash, and on his way. The goat called after the fox to remind him that he had forgotten something. The fox returned to the well for a moment and said: " Friend, if you had half as many brains as you have hairs on your chin, you would not have jumped into the well without thinking *first* about how you were going to get out."

The moral of this fable is: Think before you leap.

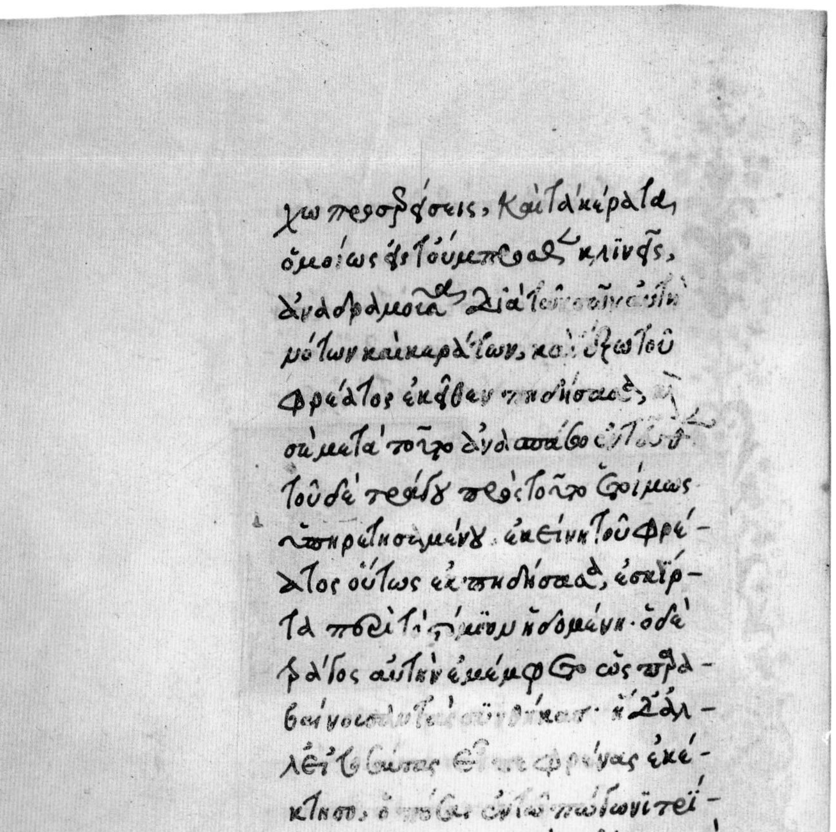

χω πρὸς ὁράσεις, καὶ τὰ λοιπὰ,
ὁμοίως δὲ τοῦ μὲν πρὸς τὰς κλίνας,
ἀναδρομὴ διὰ τῶν σωλήνων
ῥόλων καὶ παρ' αὐτῶν, καὶ ἐκ τοῦ
φρέατος ἐκ βαθέων ποιήσας, ἢ
οὐ μετὰ τοῦτο ἀναδασάμενος εἰς τὸ
τοῦ δὲ τέλει πρὸς τὸ τῶν ἑτοίμως
συγκρινομένων, ἐκείνη τοῦ φρέατος οὕτως ἐκποιήσας, ἑσπέρ-
τα πρὸς τὴν ἡμῶν ἐσομένη· ὁ δὲ
ῥάλος αὐτὴν ἔσεμφ' ὡς παρα-
βαίνοσε λυτὰ τὴν οἶκον· ἢ ἀλ-
λεῖ ὁ βίος ἔπι τε φρέγας ἐκέ-
κλισε, ὁ πάντα αὐτῷ καθ' ἑνὶ τε
γας, οὐ πρότερον ἂν καταβῆς, πρὶν
ἢ τὴν λύσιν σκέψασθαι·

Ἐπιλεύθιον·

Ὁμῶθος δηλοῖ ὅτι οὕτω καὶ
τὸν φρόνιμον ἄνδρα δεῖ πρότερον τὰ τέλη σκοπεῖν τὰ τῶν

5

THE FOX WHO HAD NEVER SEEN A LION
(Folio 5r)

Once, there was a fox who had never seen a lion. Then, by chance, he happened to come face-to-face with the king of beasts. At this first encounter, the fox was terrified.

Upon meeting the lion a second time, however, he was somewhat less afraid than before. And, by the third meeting, the fox felt so self-assured that he just sauntered up to the lion and began chatting easily with him.

The moral of this fable is: Familiarity allays fear.

f. 5r

THE WEASEL AND THE ROOSTER
(*Folios 5v–6r*)

A weasel caught a rooster but, before eating the bird, he felt a need to justify his action. So, he accused the rooster of being an annoyance to humankind by crowing early in the morning, and thereby keeping people from enjoying their sleep. The rooster retorted that he only crowed so that people would be sure to get up in time for work. The weasel thought for a moment, and then accused the rooster of incest, noting the bird's very close relationship with his mother and sisters. The rooster responded that he was only doing his job, since—thanks to him—the hens were fertile and laid many eggs. "All right," cried the frustrated weasel, "you win! You have an answer for everything!" And, with that, he ate the rooster.

The moral of this fable is: Someone intent on committing an evil act may attempt to present it in a good light—but he is not likely to change his plans if that attempt fails.

THE FOX WITH THE CROPPED TAIL
(Folios 6r–6v)

A fox who had lost his tail in a trap was so ashamed of this deformity that he felt life was no longer worth living–unless, he thought, he could convince all the other foxes to cut off *their* tails so that he wouldn't stand out as much in a crowd. To this end, he called a meeting of all the foxes and advised them to cut off their tails, since a tail was not only an ugly appendage, but it also added extra weight that had to be carried around. One of the foxes at the meeting responded skeptically: "Tell me, friend, would you be saying the same thing if *you* still had a tail?"

The moral of this fable is: When receiving "good" advice, consider the source.

THE FOX AND THE BRAMBLE
(*Folios 6v–7r*)

While climbing a fence one day, a fox lost his balance and–seeing that he was about to fall–grabbed onto a bramble to steady himself. As the thorns of the bramble cut into his paws, the fox cried out in pain: "I reached out to you for help, and you have only made the situation worse!" "You were mistaken," responded the bramble, "when you tried to catch hold of me. My thorns are there to catch others."

The moral of this fable is: If you are in need of a friend, don't seek out someone more likely to hurt than to help.

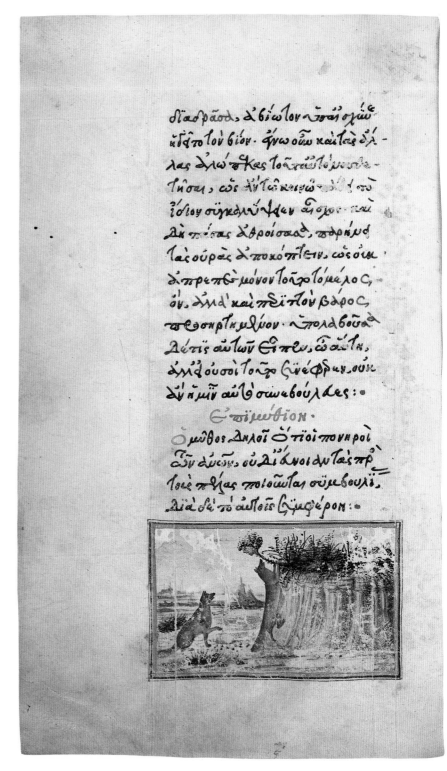

7

THE FOX AND THE CROCODILE
(*Folios 7r–7v*)

A fox and a crocodile were arguing over the distinction of their respective lineages. The crocodile went on at great length about his illustrious ancestors, concluding his monologue with the boast that one of his forefathers had been a distinguished trainer, responsible for conditioning the best athletes. This was just too much for the exasperated fox, who hissed: "You could have spared yourself the trouble of mentioning that last point. By the look of your hide, it's obvious you haven't derived much benefit from any time *you've* spent in the gymnasium."

The moral of this fable is: Like crocodiles, like men—liars often give themselves away.

THE ROOSTERS AND THE PARTRIDGE

(Folios 7v–8r)

One day, a farmer bought a partridge to raise among his roosters. The roosters, however, did not take kindly to the newcomer—they pecked at her and chased her around the barnyard from morning to night. The partridge was saddened by this, thinking she was being persecuted because she was a bird of a different feather. But, after a while, she began to notice that the roosters were as mean-tempered toward one another as they were toward her. Sometimes, they fought so intensely among themselves that they actually drew blood. Seeing this, she said to herself: "Well, I really can't complain about the way they treat me, since they treat each other the same way—if not worse."

The moral of this fable is: So, too, even wise men may be willing to tolerate abuse when they see that it is widespread.

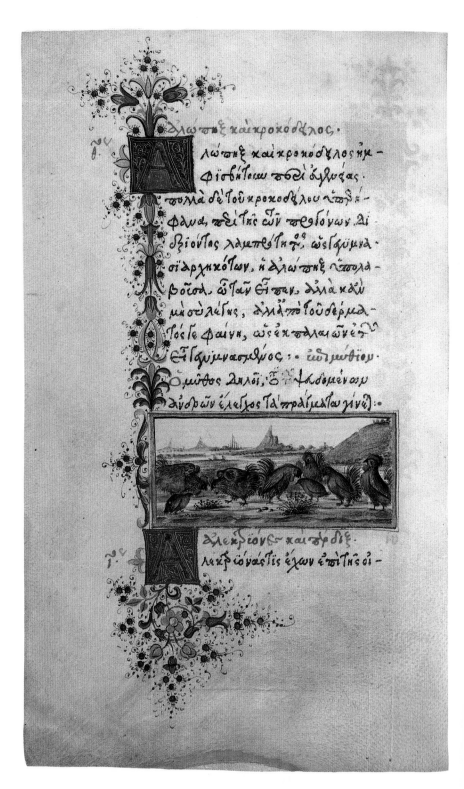

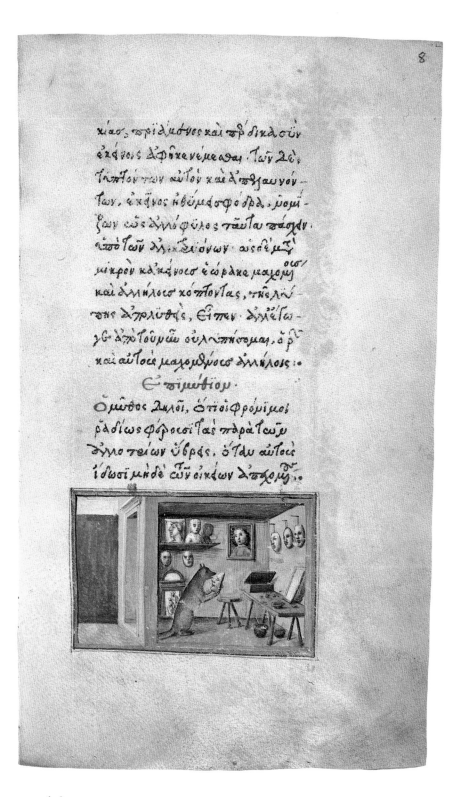

f. 8r

THE FOX AND THE MASK
(Folios 8r–8v)

A fox managed to find his way into an actor's house one day. He was having a wonderful time rummaging through the actor's belongings, when he discovered a mask of the type used in theatrical performances. It was beautifully made and the fox was completely captivated. He held it up in his paws and gazed raptly at it. "Such a lovely face," he said to himself, "what a pity it doesn't have a brain to go with it."

The moral of this fable is: Too often, a pretty face masks an empty head.

THE COAL MAN AND THE FULLER

(Folios 8v–9r)

There was once a coal man who had a large house all to himself–far more room than he really needed. So, he looked around for someone with whom to share his home. Noticing that a fuller had set up shop nearby, the coal man went and asked him if he would like to join forces. By sharing a house, he told the fuller, both of them would have the advantages of companionship and, in addition, two could live as cheaply as one. The fuller, however, rejected the offer immediately. "It's obvious that such an arrangement really would not be suitable," he told the coal man, "for everything which I strive to make white, you would blacken with your soot."

The moral of this fable is: Birds of an obviously different feather should nest separately.

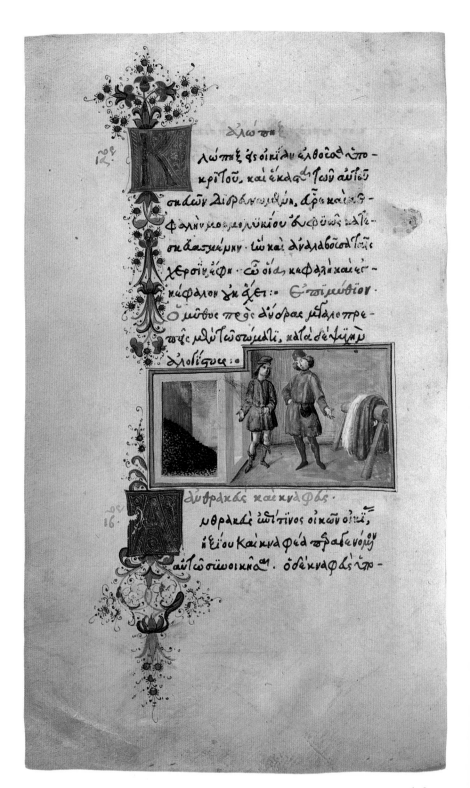

f. 8v

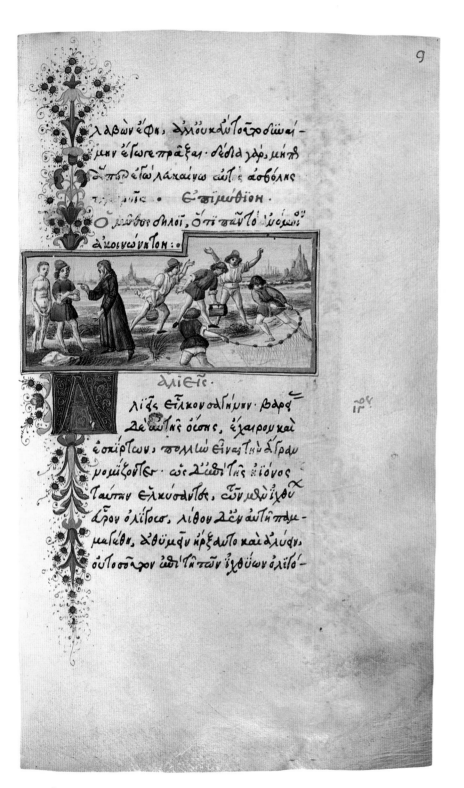

f. 9r

THE FISHERMEN WHO CAUGHT STONES
(Folios 9r–9v)

As they dragged their nets through the sea, a group of fishermen felt them growing suddenly heavy. Assuming that they had trapped a whole school of fish, they became deliriously happy. But, no sooner had they dragged the nets onto the shore than their joy evaporated, for there was nothing in the nets but large rocks and flotsam. They became very depressed, as much by their foolhardy optimism as by the stark reality of their "catch." But their dejection was not unanimous. One experienced old salt said to his mates: "Don't be so downcast, my friends. Joy and sadness are close relations. Because our sense of triumph was so great, it made our disappointment that much more deeply felt."

The moral of this fable is: So, too, we can expect that any beautiful day may be brought to an abrupt end by a violent storm.

THE BRAGGART

(Folios 9v–10r)

There was a professional athlete whose
talents were not exactly world class, to
say the least, and the same was true of his
mind. Indeed, his fellow citizens often
mocked his abilities. After he returned
from a trip abroad one year, he began to
brag about his athletic triumphs while
on the road. He was particularly proud,
he claimed, of a jump he had made on
the island of Rhodes. To hear him tell
it, he had jumped higher and farther than
anyone ever had before—no Olympic
athlete could hope to match his leap.
Rather smugly, he said that, if anyone
doubted him, they could confirm his
claim the next time anyone came through
town who was from Rhodes. "But excuse me," said one of those who had
been listening to the athlete's self-
aggrandizement. "Here's a spot that's
just as good as the one on Rhodes. So
let's see you jump."

The moral of this fable is: Actions speak
louder (sometimes—but, in any case,
always more convincingly) than words.

10

THE MAN WHO PROMISED THE IMPOSSIBLE
(*Folios 10r–10v*)

A poor man was so sick that he was almost at death's door. Since his doctors offered him no hope of survival, he turned to the gods, imploring their aid. He promised to make an impressive sacrifice and to build a special shrine to all the gods, if they would only help him recover. The man's wife, hearing this vow, asked him: "Where will the money come from to pay for all these promises, if you should get better?" To which her husband replied: "Do you think I can afford to worry about my debt to the gods while I'm in this condition?"

The moral of this fable is: When they find themselves in desperate straits, some people will try any stratagem in their efforts to save themselves.

THE CHEAT

(Folios 10v–11r)

A cheat made a bet with another man
that he could prove the Delphic oracle a
liar. So, one day, he caught a sparrow,
hid it beneath his cloak, and entered the
temple. Standing before the oracle, he
asked whether the object in his hand was
dead or alive. If the oracle said "dead,"
he planned to present the living bird.
If the oracle said "alive," he intended to
strangle the bird and present the corpse
instead. But the oracle saw through this
ruse and replied: "Why ask me, you
rogue, when you know quite well the
answer to your question."

The moral of this fable is: You can fool
some of the people all of the time, but
you cannot fool the gods.

ςρουτίον ἐντῇ χΔεῖ. καὶ τὸ χρτ τῆε ἀδη -
λίου ἐπα᾽ζω, ἐσαῖε τοῦ ξίποδος
ἥμισυ· καὶ ἦρ ᾽ζω τὸν θεὸν λέγων,
ἀ᾽ῶλλον, ὁ μεΔὶ χεῖρασ φέρω,
τόδρον ἐ᾽ρπνοαν ἐσὶν ἢ ἄ᾽πνοαν,
βουλόμευος, ὡς ᾽ἢ μὲν ἄ᾽πνοαν εἴ -
πω. ζῶν Δὺ ἀ᾽ΔᾷξαιΤὸ ςρουτίον· ἢ
Δὰξᾷ ᾽πνοαν, ἄποᾷ ᾽πο πνίξας, νε -
κρὸν ἐκεῖνο περ χᾷ χρᾶν· ὁ δέ γε
θεὸς Τὴν χακό Τεχνον αὐτοῦ γνὸς ἐ -
πίνοιαδν, εἶπεν· ὁ πόλρον ὦ οὗ -
Τος βούλᾷ ᾽ποιήσαι, ᾽ποίησον· ᾽πρὰ σὶ
χεῖ Ται γὰρ Τὸ χρτ ᾽πρᾶξαι, ἢ Τοι ζῆν
ὁ ᾽κα Τέχεις ἢ νεκρὸν ᾽ποδᾷξαι:·

Ε᾽πιμ᾽ύθιον.

Ὁ μῦθος Δηλοῖ, ὅτι Τὸ θᾷον ἄ᾽πα -
ράλο᾽γισον καὶ ἀ᾽λάθητον:·

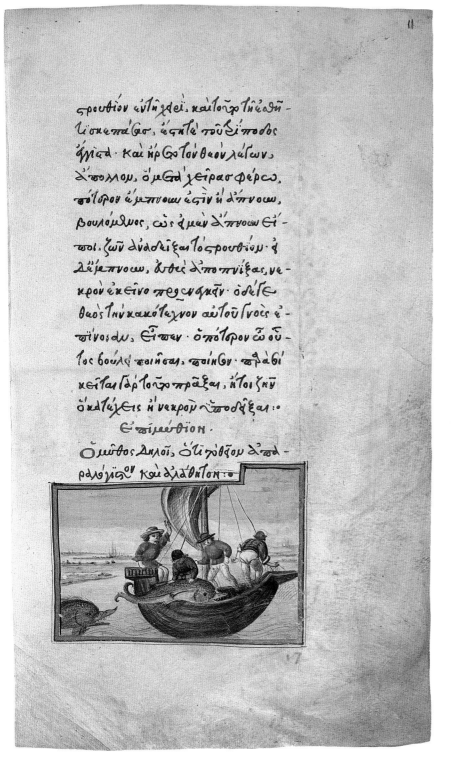

THE FISHERMEN AND THE TUNA
(Folios 11r–11v)

A boatload of fishermen had been at sea for an entire day with only empty nets to show for all their efforts. Finally, they decided it was useless to continue, and they turned their boat toward home. At that very moment, a huge tuna fish—fleeing in panic from some underwater foe—jumped right onto their deck. So, they returned to port with a fine catch after all, and sold the tuna at a very good price.

The moral of this fable is: Thus does chance often bestow the prize that time and trouble have failed to achieve.

39

THE BROKEN VOW
(*Folios 11v–12v*)

Once there was a poor man who was mortally ill. He prayed to the gods, promising that he would sacrifice one hundred oxen to them in gratitude, if only they would spare his life. The gods decided to put him to the test. He quickly recovered from his illness and was up and about in no time. Then he remembered that he had neither the one hundred oxen due the gods, nor the money with which to buy them. After much thought, he did what he considered to be the next best thing–he modeled one hundred oxen in wax and sacrificed them on an altar with the prayer: "Here, Oh gods, is the offering that I promised."

The gods were not amused. To avenge themselves, they sent the man a dream

f. 11v

θεοῖς ἐδίδου δἐκ βοῦς ἐκατὸν εἰς
θυσίαν προσοίσειν. οἱ δὲ θεοὶ πειρᾶ-
σαι τοῦτον βουλόμενοι. Τοῦ πλάθεος
ἀπήλλαξαν. ὁ δὲ ἀναστὰς, ἐπ̓ ᾐ δὴ'
βοῶν ἢ πορᾷ, τὰ δὲ τίνους βοῦς ἐκα-
τον πλέας ἰδὼν τοῦ βωμοῦ θὰς ὡλο-
καύτωσεν. οἱ δὲ θεοὶ βουλόμενοι
αὐτὸν ἀμείψασθαι, ὄναρ αὐτῷ ἰδόν-
τες αὐτῷ εἶπον. ἀπελθὼ εἰς τὸν
αἰγιαλὸν ἐς τόνδε τὸν τόπον. εὑρή-
σει ἀττικὰς χιλίας δραχμὰς. ἐπ̓
μεσθεὶς ἐπὶ τῷ ἰδών, ἐπὶ ἡ δονὴ καὶ
πορεύθη πρὸς τὸν ἀποδειχθέντα τόπον φίκελο. τὸ χρυσίον διαρθρῶν.
ἐπὶ δὲ δι πειραταῖς τισι τῶν, ὑ
παῦτων συνελήφθη. δ̓ οἷς δὲ ὐ
δη. ἀφεθῆναι τῶν πειρατῶν ἐδεῖ-
το. χιλία χρυσίου τάλαν τὸ δ̓ ωσόν
αὐτοῖς ἀπιγνώμενος. αὐτῶ δ̓
οὐκ ἀπιδέκλειο. ἀπαχθεὶς ἐπ̓ αὐτ-

in which he was walking by the seashore and found 1,000 drachmas lying on the sand. When he awoke, he ran down to the beach, scarcely able to contain his joy at such impending good fortune. He was met there, however, by a band of pirates who carried him off and sold him into slavery. The price he brought: 1,000 drachmas.

The moral of this fable is: Beware of making promises to the gods, for they will expect you to fulfill them to the letter.

THE FROGS AND THE DRIED-UP POND

(Folios 12v–13r)

There were two frogs living happily in a pond. As summer came to an end, however, the pond dried up, so they had to leave in search of another place to live. Soon, they came to a deep well. One frog said to the other: "Friend, let's make our home down in this well." The other answered: "And if this well should dry up, just as the pond did, how will we ever be able to get back up?"

The moral of this fable is: Beware of impulsive decisions.

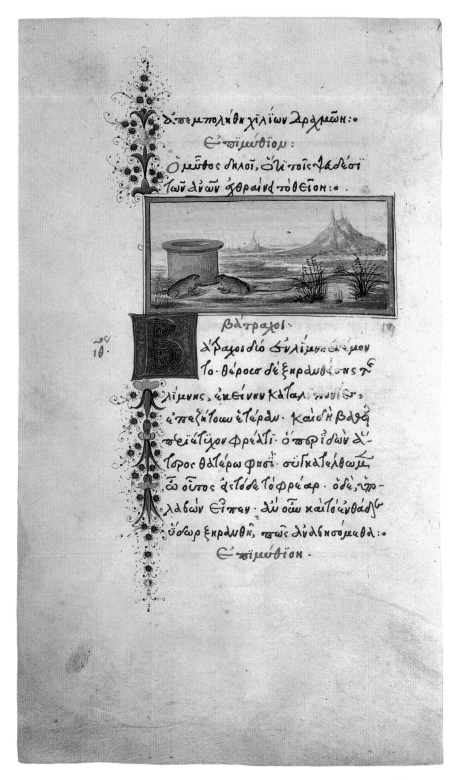

f. 12v

42

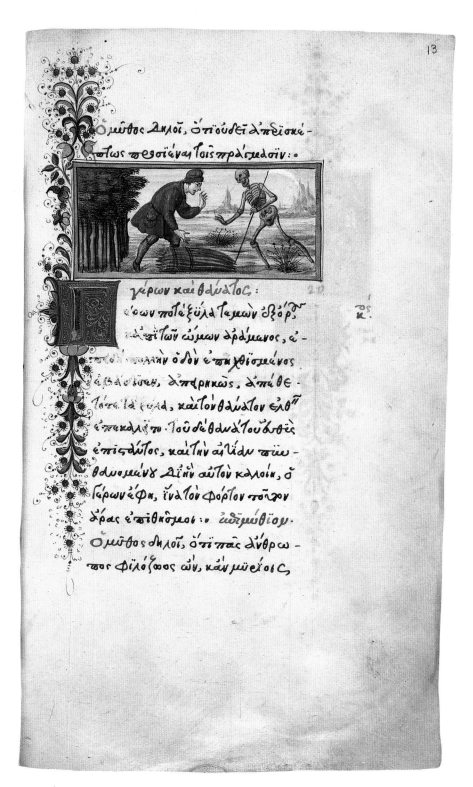

13

THE OLD MAN AND DEATH
(Folios 13r–13v)

One day, an old man was out chopping wood in the forest. When he had cut a big stack, he packed it up and lifted it onto his back. But he was far from home and, as he trudged along, he became very weary. Finally, in despair, he lowered his burden to the ground and summoned death. Death appeared and asked the old man what he wanted. Pointing to the wood, the old man replied: "I want you to carry this for me."

The moral of this fable is: Life, any sort of life, is preferable to the alternative.

THE OLD WOMAN AND THE DOCTOR

(Folios 13v–14v)

There was an old woman who was having trouble with her eyes. She summoned a doctor, and agreed to pay him once she was cured. The doctor came to her house to begin the treatment, which consisted of applying a salve over a period of weeks. Each time he came, he would steal something from her house while her eyes were covered with the medicine. In time, the cure was completed, and so was the doctor's theft of all his patient's household goods. Naturally, he expected to be paid for his services, as they had agreed.

The old woman, however, refused to pay the doctor, and so he took her to court. In front of the judge, the old woman admitted that she had promised to pay the doctor upon the completion of the cure. But, actually, she told the judge, her condition had become worse: "Before the doctor began his treatment I could see all the furniture in my house, and now I can't see a single piece!"

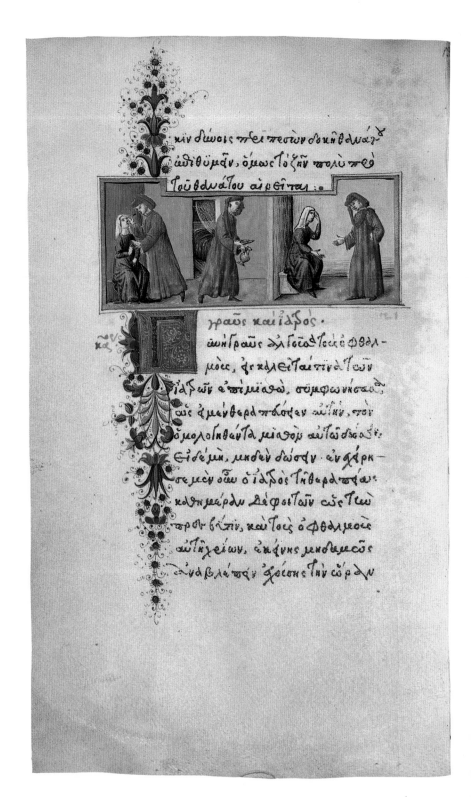

14

The moral of this fable is: A thief will often supply the necessary evidence for his own conviction.

ἐκλύην ἀπὸ τοῦ χρυσοχ γ̇: αὐτὸς
ἐκ τῆς τῆς οἰκίας σκεύη ἀφαι-
ρούμενος, ὃ σημέρα ἀπ. τ̇: τί
μὲν οὖν ἔρας τὴν ἑαυτῆς ποι-
οσοίδι ἑώρα καθ ἑκάστην ἐλατ-
μένην ἀπὸ τοσοῦτον, ὡς καὶ τέλος
τῶν ἐπασσοῖν αὐτῆ θεραπᾶσθαι ὅ
μηδὲν ἀπολιφθῆναι. τοῦ δὲ δ̇ ϸ̇
τοῖς συμφωνηθείσας μισθοῖς
εἰ μὲν δ̇ πάντος ἐῶντος αὐ ἐκδαρϸ̇
βλέπουσιν ἣ δια, καὶ τοῖς μάρτυ-
ρας παραλαβόντος, μᾶλλον μὲν
οὖν ἔϊ πάντ ἐκδύνη τὰ νῶν οὐ δ̇λ̇-
σω βλέπω: ἣ νίκα μὲν γὰρ τοῖς ὀ-
φθαλμοὶς ἐνόσουν, πολλὰ τῶν
ἐμῶν κατὰ τὴν ἐμαυτῆς ἔβλεπ
οἰκίαν. νῦν δ' ὅτε με οὐ βλέπ
φῆς, οὐδ' ἓν ἐκδύνην ὁρῶ :·

Ἐπιμύθιον.

Ὁ μῦθος δηλοῖ, ὅτι οἱ πονηροὶ

THE FARMER AND HIS CHILDREN

(Folios 14v–15r)

On his deathbed, a farmer wished to bestow upon his children their rightful inheritance. He called them to his side and said: "My children, I am about to depart from this world. Look in the vineyard and you will find there the treasure I have hidden for you." He passed away and, immediately, his heirs began digging furiously around the vines. They failed to find any buried treasure, but the vines–improved by all the digging–produced more grapes that year than they ever had before.

The moral of this fable is: Work is humanity's greatest treasure.

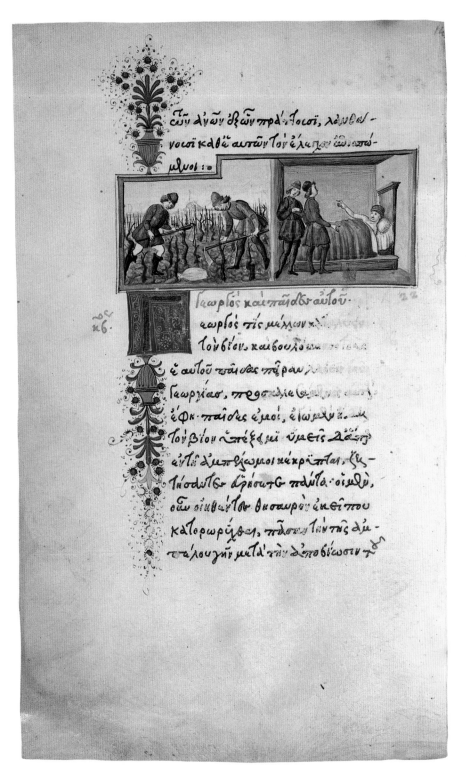

f. 14v

46

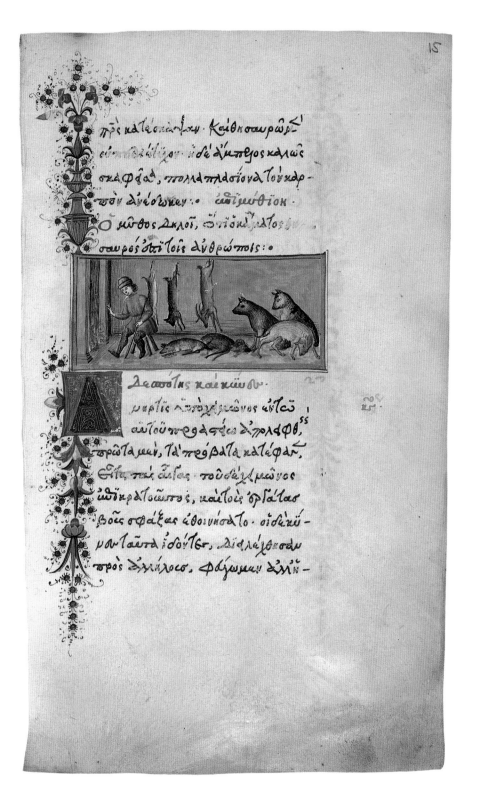

15

THE FARMER AND HIS DOGS
(*Folios 15r–15v*)

A terrible winter imprisoned a farmer on his own farm. Since he could not leave his home to seek food elsewhere, he began to eat his livestock. First, he ate the sheep. Then, as the bad weather continued, he ate the goats as well. When there was still no end to the miserable season, he finally ate the oxen who pulled his plow.

His dogs noticed the disappearance of their fellow animals one by one, and they became alarmed. "We had better leave while we still can," they said to one another. "If the farmer was desperate enough to kill and eat the oxen he needs for his work in the fields, why should we expect him to spare us?" And so, they ran off.

The moral of this fable is: One must be wary of those whose only concern is for their own welfare.

THE WOMAN AND THE HEN
(Folios 15v–16r)

An old woman had a hen who laid one egg every day. Not satisfied with this level of production, the woman decided that, if she increased the hen's rations, the obliging creature should be able to lay at least two eggs a day. So, the old woman began to stuff the hen full of food. In time, the hen became so overfed and lethargic that she couldn't even lay her one egg!

The moral of this fable is: Despite rumors to the contrary, greed is not good.

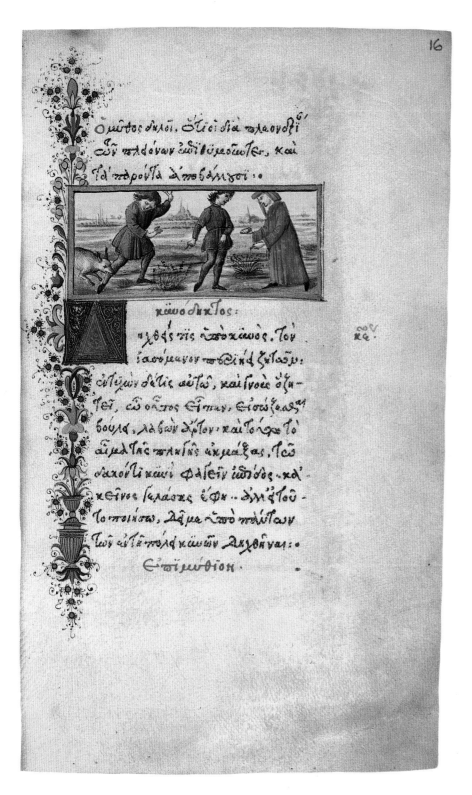

16

ΟΜΕΝΤΟC ΔΗΛΟΙ ΟΤΙ ΟΙ ΔΙΑ ΠΛΕΟΝΕΞΙ·
ΤΩΝ ΠΛΕΙΟΝΩΝ ΕΦΙΕΜΕΝΟΙΤΕ, ΚΑΙ
ΤΑ ΠΑΡΟΝΤΑ ΑΠΟΒΑΛΛΟΥΣΙ·

ΚΥΝΟ ΔΗΚΤΟC·

ΔΗΧΘΕΙC ΤΙC ΥΠΟ ΚΥΝΟC. Περι·
ΗΕΙ ΖΗΤΩΝ ΤΟΝ ΙΑCΟΜΕΝΟΝ·

DOG BITES MAN
(*Folios 16r–16v*)

A man was bitten by a dog and went feverishly in search of someone to treat the wound. One helpful soul told him that all he had to do to stop the flow of blood was to staunch it with a piece of bread and then, when the bread was soaked with blood, toss it to the dog who had bitten him. "That sounds like a good way," answered the man, "to ensure that I'll be torn to pieces by every dog in town."

The moral of this fable is: So, too, with men–reward their wickedness and they will make a habit of it.

THE TWO BOYS AND THE BUTCHER

(Folios 16v–17r)

Two young boys went to buy meat at a butcher's shop. Seeing that the butcher was busy helping a customer, one of the boys grabbed a piece of beef and stuffed it down the shirt of the other. The butcher, having finished serving his customer, came over to where the boys were standing and immediately noticed that some beef was missing. He accused the boys of theft, but the one who had taken it said that he didn't have it, and the one who had it said that he hadn't taken it. The butcher understood their trickery and warned them: "You may think you can get away with this bit of double-talk here, but the gods won't be deceived by such sophistry."

The moral of this fable is: Sometimes lying and telling the literal truth can amount to the same thing.

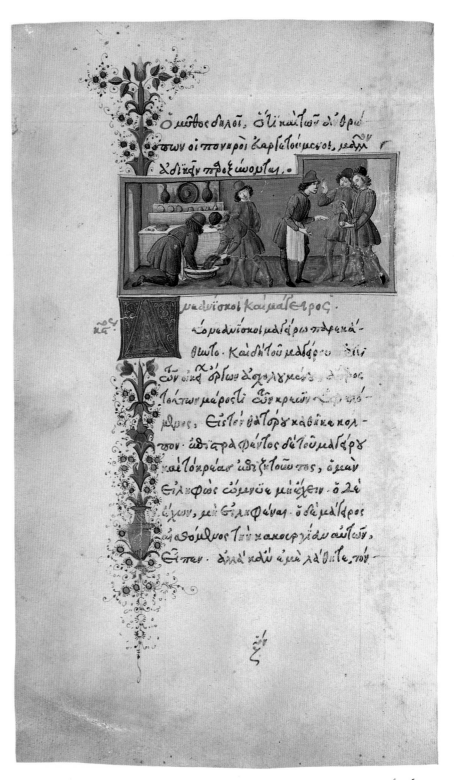

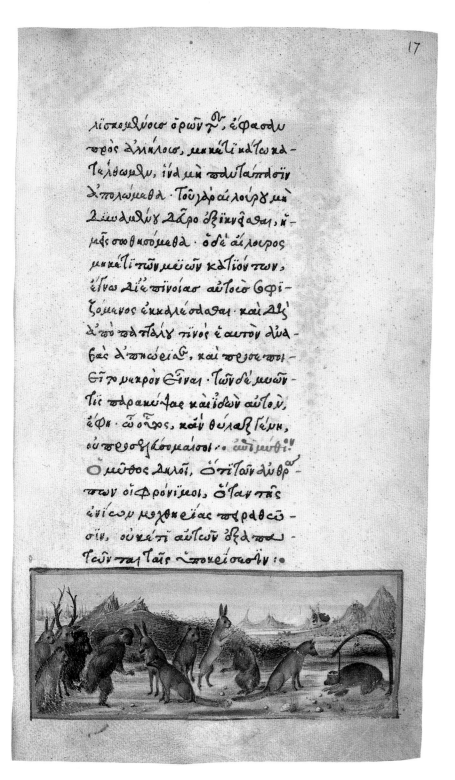

17

THE FOX AND THE MONKEY KING

(Folios 17r–18r)

A monkey had so impressed and delighted his fellow animals by dancing for them at a party that they agreed he should be their king. A fox became jealous of this honor, and decided to teach the monkey a lesson. He told the monkey that he had found a great treasure and, rather than keep it for himself, he wished to present it—out of deference—to his king. In fact, this "treasure" was no more than a piece of meat set as bait in a trap. The monkey, his head swollen with false pride, carelessly reached for the bait and was instantly caught in the trap. He began to curse the fox for having tricked him. The fox replied: "Majesty, idiot that you are, can you really imagine yourself worthy to be king of all animals?"

The moral of this fable is: So, too, with those who undertake tasks for which they are clearly not qualified—they run the risk not only of failure but also of making complete fools of themselves.

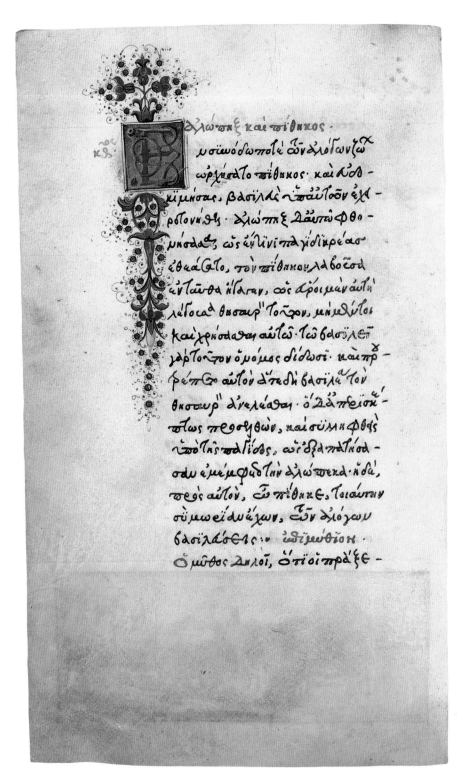

Ἀλώπηξ καὶ πίθηκος·

Ἐν συνόδῳ τῶν ἀλόγων ζῴ-
ων ὠρχήσατο πίθηκος· καὶ εὐδο-
κιμήσας, βασιλεὺς ὑπ' αὐτῶν ἐχει-
ροτονήθη· Ἀλώπηξ δὲ αὐτῷ φθο-
νήσασα, ὡς ἔν τινι πάγῃ κρέας
ἐθεάσατο, τὸν πίθηκον λαβοῦσα
ἐνταῦθα ἤγαγεν, ὡς εὑροῦσα αὐτὴ
λέγουσα θησαυρὸν τοῦτον, μὴ ἐδηλώθη
καὶ ἐχρήσατο αὐτῷ. τῷ βασιλεῖ
γὰρ τοῦτον ὁ νόμος δίδωσι· καὶ παρ-
ῄνει ὡς αὐτὸν ὅτι δὴ βασιλεῖ τὸν
θησαυρὸν ἀνελέσθαι. ὁ δὲ ἀπερισκέπ-
τως προσελθὼν, καὶ συνελήφθη
ὑπὸ τῆς πάγης, ὡς δὲ ἀπατηθεὶς
ἐμέμφετο τὴν ἀλώπεκα· ἡ δὲ
πρὸς αὐτόν· ὦ πίθηκε, τοιαύτην
σὺ μωρίαν ἔχων, τῶν ἀλόγων
βασιλεύεις;·· ἐπιμύθιον·
Ὁ μῦθος δηλοῖ, ὅτι οἱ πράξε-

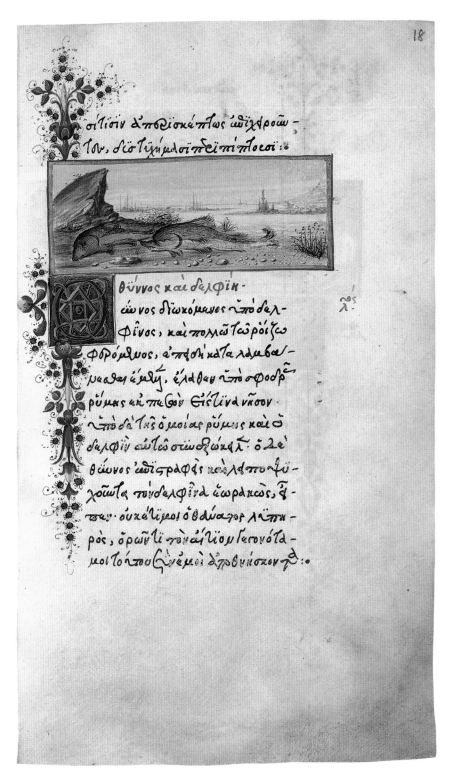

18

THE TUNA AND THE DOLPHIN
(Folios 18r–18v)

A tuna was being chased through the sea by a dolphin. After a long and wearying chase, the tuna was on the verge of being captured when the momentum of his final leap caused him to land on the shore. In hot pursuit, the dolphin followed, and so they were both stranded. Watching the dolphin breathe his last, the tuna said: "I have no dread of death now, since I see that the one who threatened my life has lost his own."

The moral of this fable is: One is better able to bear misfortunes when they are shared by those who have caused them.

f. 18r

THE DOCTOR AND HIS PATIENT
(Folios 18v–19r)

When one of his patients died, the man's doctor attended the funeral. There, he delivered a eulogy, noting: "If the deceased had abstained from wine and taken his medicine instead, he would be alive today." One of the mourners was annoyed by this lack of feeling, and spoke up: "It seems to me that it's a little late for this kind of diagnosis—you ought to have told the dead man when it might still have done him some good."

The moral of this fable is: It is better to help one's friends when they are in need, than to offer them good advice when they are long past caring.

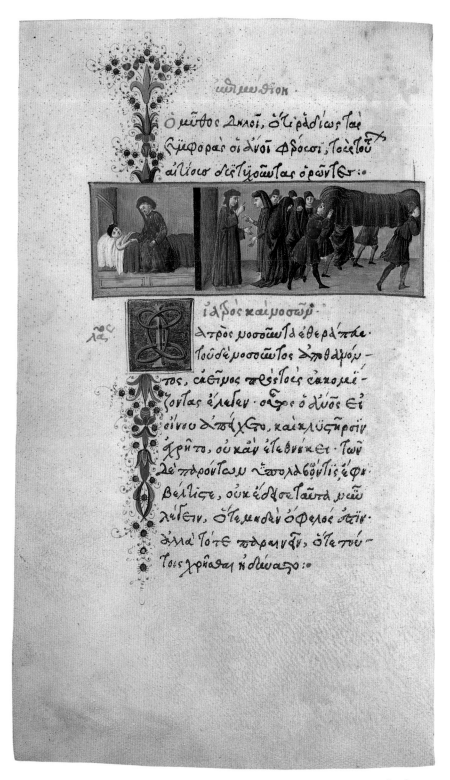

f. 19r

THE BIRD CATCHER AND THE VIPER
(Folios 19r–19v)

A bird catcher set forth one day, armed with bait and traps. He caught sight of a thrush high up in a tree and decided to try to catch it. He began assembling his trap, attaching it to several sticks so that it would reach the bird, but–while he was busily at work, concentrating on the prey high above his head–he failed to notice where he was stepping, and he tripped over a sleeping viper. Taking umbrage at being so rudely wakened, the snake bit the bird catcher. Sensing that the end was near, the bird catcher cried out: "Oh, unfortunate wretch that I am, I was so intent upon my prey I couldn't see the lurking danger that made me another's prey."

The moral of this fable is: So, too, with those who lay traps for other people–they sometimes find themselves more preyed upon than preying.

THE CASTOR

(*Folios 19v–20r*)

Castors are four-legged creatures who live
in ponds. Their private parts are said by
some to be useful in curing certain ill-
nesses. And so, when people see one and
begin to give chase, the castor knows
exactly what it is they want and flees
as fast as he can run. But, if his pursuers
are gaining on him, he stops, rips off
what they are after, and throws them to
his would-be captors. Thus, he saves
his life.

The moral of this fable is: When their
lives are threatened because they possess
a great treasure, men are wise to sacrifice
their jewels to save their lives.

κατααλαμβανω), γινωσκων ου χειν
διωκω, αρτεμων τα εαυτου αε-
δοια ειπι προς τος διωκονas.
και ουτω σωτηειας τυχανει:·

Επιμυθιον.

Ο μυθος διλοι, οτι ουτω και τ
ανων οι φρονιμοι τωρ της εαυτ
σωτηειας ουδενα λογον των χρη-
ματων ποιουνται:·

κυων και μαγειρος.
υων εις πηδησας ας μαγα-
ρᾶον, και του μαγαιρχ αρχο-
λουμενου, καρδίαν αρπασας εφ
φυγεν. ο δε μαγαρος επιστραφεις,
ως ειδεν αυτον φευγοντα ειπεν.

f. 20r

THE DOG AND THE BUTCHER
(*Folios 20r–20v*)

A dog slipped into a butcher shop when the butcher wasn't looking, snatched a beef heart, and fled. The butcher saw the dog's tail as he ran out the door, and shouted: "Don't worry, you thief, wherever you go I'll find you and give you what you deserve, for you haven't so much stolen a heart as actually given me heart."

The moral of this fable is: Although accidents can always happen, sometimes they may prove useful.

THE SLEEPING DOG AND THE WOLF

(Folios 20v–21r)

A dog was sleeping peacefully in a court-yard. Along came a wolf who saw this easy prey and leaped on him, intending to make the dog his dinner. Politely, the dog asked the wolf not to eat him just then, pointing out that he was nothing but a bag of bones. If the wolf would only return in a few weeks, the dog claimed, he would find a more substantial meal awaiting him. The dog explained the reason for this–his owners were going to have a wedding celebration soon and there would be many leftovers for him to eat. The wolf thought this sounded plausible, so he released the dog and departed. A few weeks later he came back, looking for the dog. He finally saw him sleeping on the house's highest ledge. He called to the dog and reminded him of their previous conversation. The dog replied: "Wolf, old friend, if–in the future–you should find me sleeping down there in the courtyard, don't wait for another wedding."

The moral of this fable is: People will tell any tale to protect their lives.

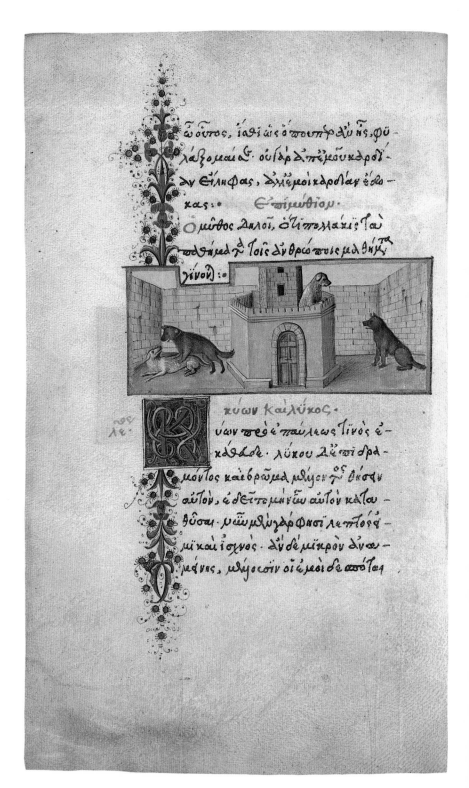

σοις ἐφυσᾶ μοσο· καὶ τῶ Ἰκανικῶσ τὰ πολλὰ φαγῶν, πιμελώτερος ἔσομαι· ἢ
σοὶ κ δῦ βον βρῶμα γενήσομαι· ὁ
μὲ σπιλύκος ταῦ εἰς ἀπῆλθε
μὰ ἡμέρας ὰ ἐπανελθῶν, ἄρον
ὰ νεσ ἰδὶ Ιοῦ δομα τ Ιοῦ κὼσ α κα
δ᾽ ιδόντ· καὶ σὰς καὶ ιωβεν, πρὸς
ὰ αυτὸν ἐκάλα, τῶ μιμνήσκων
αὐτὸν αὐῦ σιω θακῶν· καὶ ὁ κύ,
ἀνῶ λύκα, ἐτο ἀπο Ιοῦ δὲ πρὸ τῆς
Ιοαύλεως με ι δοις καθ᾽ λιοδύ̈λα, κα
κά τέ τὰ μοις ἀναμεῖνης · ιω̈ῦ με
ὁ μῦθος δηλοῖ, ὅτι οἱ φρονίμοι
ῶν ἀνῶν ὅ Ιαν πεῖ τι κίνδυ ᾽δι-
σωθῶσι, διὰ βίου Ιοῦ πρ φυ-
λάντ ιονται · ·

THE DOG, THE ROOSTER, AND THE FOX
(Folios 21r–22r)

A dog and a rooster, who had become friends, went out together for a walk along the road. As night fell, the rooster flew up into a tree to find a perch upon which to sleep, and the dog crawled into a hollow at the base of the tree to do the same. When morning came, the rooster crowed his usual greeting, attracting the attention of a fox. The fox called up to the rooster, asking him to come down, so that he could congratulate the rooster personally for having such a beautiful voice. The rooster suggested to the fox that he awaken the "doorman" who slept at the foot of the tree–the rooster said he would come down when the "doorman" opened the door. The fox went searching around the base of the tree to find the "doorman," who promptly pounced on the fox and tore him to pieces.

The moral of this fable is: In dangerous circumstances, sensible people always make sure that they have big, strong friends around to protect them.

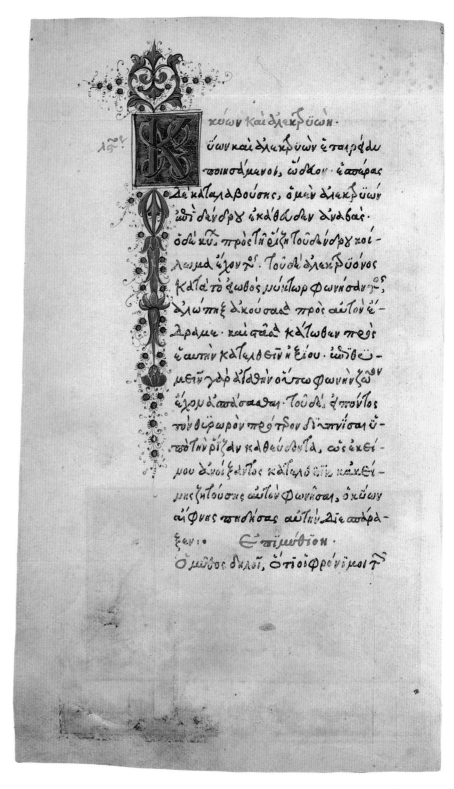

κύων καὶ ἀλεκτρυών·

Κύων καὶ ἀλεκτρυὼν ἑταιρίαν
ποιησάμενοι, ὡδοίπορον· ἑσπέρας
δὲ καταλαβούσης, ὁ μὲν ἀλεκτρυὼν
ἐπὶ δάνδρου ἐκάθισεν ἀναβαὶς.
ὁ δὲ κύ. πρὸς τῇ ῥίζῃ τοῦ δένδρου κοί
λωμα ἔχον γ. Τοῦ δὲ ἀλεκτρυόνος
κατὰ τὸ ἔωθος μέντοι φωνήσαντος,
ἀλώπηξ ἀκούσασα πρὸς αὐτὸν ἔ
δραμε· καὶ στᾶσα κάτωθεν πρὸς
ἑαυτὴν κατελθεῖν ἠξίου. ἐπιθε
μεῖν γὰρ ἀγαθὸν οὕτω φωνὴν ἔχον
τι ζῶον ἀσπάσασθαι. Τοῦ δὲ εἰπόντος
τὸν θυρωρὸν πρό τερον διυπνίσαι ὑ
πὸ τὴν ῥίζαν καθεύδοντα, ὡς ἐκεῖ
νου ἀνοίξαντος κατελθεῖν· κἀκεί
νης ζητούσης αὐτὸν φωνῆσαι, ὁ κύων
αἴφνης πηδήσας αὐτὴν διεσπάρα
ξεν:· Ἐπιμύθιον·
ὁ μῦθος δηλοῖ, ὅτι οἱ φρόνιμοι τ

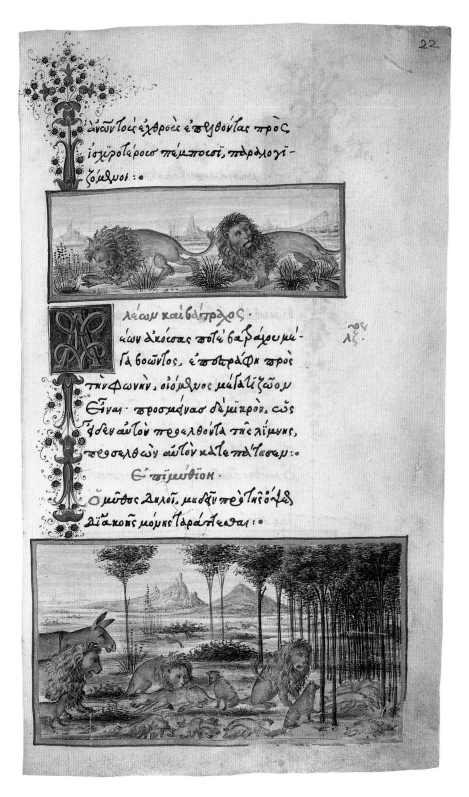

f. 22r

THE LION AND THE FROG
(*Folio 22r*)

A lion was intrigued by the croaking of a frog, a sound he had never heard before. From its great volume, he assumed that it must be a sound made by some large animal. So, he went over to the pond where the noise was loudest, looking for this creature. When he saw the frog leaping from the water onto the land, he went up to it and crushed it with his heavy paw. His parting words to the lifeless frog were: "Such a little body, and such a big mouth."

The moral of this fable is: Loudmouths should take note of the frog's fate.

THE LION, THE DONKEY, AND THE FOX
(*Folios 22r–22v*)

A lion, a donkey, and a fox (having become friends) went out hunting together. When they had caught a great quantity of game, the lion asked the donkey to divide up the spoils. The donkey made three equal piles of the slaughtered animals, and asked the lion to choose the one he wanted. The lion, angered by this act of lese-majesté, promptly pounced upon the hapless donkey, and devoured him. Then, turning to the fox, the lion asked him to make the division. The fox gathered all the prey together in a single pile, reserving for himself only a few mean scraps. Bowing to the lion, he asked the king of beasts to choose one. The lion asked the fox how he had learned to divide so well. The fox replied: "By observing the donkey's fate."

The moral of this fable is: A wise man learns from the misfortunes of his neighbors.

THE LION, THE BEAR, AND THE FOX
(Folios 22v–23r)

A lion and a bear met in the woods where the body of a fawn lay waiting to be devoured. They immediately began fighting for possession of the prey, striking one another with fearsome blows, while they roared and growled loudly. They fought so long and so hard that they were both nearly at death's door when a fox—who had heard the com-

f. 22v

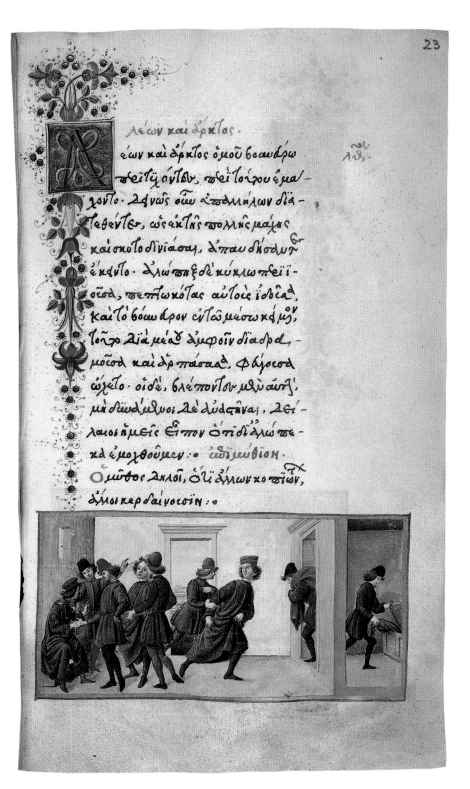

motion—passed by. Seeing that the two mighty beasts were incapacitated, the fox pounced on the fawn and dragged it off. The lion and the bear looked up from the ground upon which they lay prostrate, and moaned: "Oh, what unfortunate creatures are we, to have expended so much energy on behalf of the fox."

The moral of this fable is: One may be justifiably annoyed when those who have done no work profit from one's labors.

THE FORTUNE-TELLER
(*Folios 23r–23v*)

A fortune-teller had set up shop in a public square and was forecasting the future for anyone willing to pay his fee. Soon, a man came along and told the fortune-teller that the doors of his house were wide open and all his possessions had been stolen. Greatly agitated, the fortune-teller jumped up, crying to the man that he had to see for himself what had happened. To which the man replied: "You take other people's money, claiming that you can give them a glimpse of what is to come, and yet you can't even foresee your own fate!"

f. 23r

The moral of this fable is: Beware of those who are incapable of keeping their own lives in order, yet presume to tell others what they should do.

THE ANT AND THE DOVE
(*Folios 23v–24r*)

An ant was so thirsty that he threw caution to the winds and jumped into a stream to drink his fill. But he had not taken the water's strong current into account and was on the verge of drowning when a dove, flying by, happened to notice the ant's struggles. Plucking a twig from a nearby tree, the dove dropped it into the stream and the ant scrambled onto this "raft," which floated him safely to shore. When the ant reached the bank of the stream, he saw that a bird catcher was creeping up behind the dove, preparing to snare the bird. The ant scurried over to the man and bit him on the foot. Startled, the man dropped his net, and the dove flew off.

The moral of this fable is: One should repay good deeds in kind.

f. 23v

μύρμηξ καὶ πεῖσρά.

ύρμηξ δ'ι'ψήσας, καὶ ελθὼν δὲ
σπήν, παρα σύρδς ὑπὸ τοῦ
ρεύμα τος ἀπεπνίγετο. πεῖσρά
δὲ τοῦτο θεασαμένη, κλῶνα δαψιλῆ
σειλεσεῦ, ἐς τὴν πηγὴν ἔρριψεν.
ἐφ'οῦ καὶ καθίσας ὁ μύρμηξ δι-ε-
σώθη. ἰξδ'τὴς δέ τις μετὰ τὸ γο
τοὶς καλάμοις σιωπῇ, ἐπὶ τὸ τῶ
πεῖσρὰν σὐλλαβεῖν ἦει. τὸ γο
δ'ὁ μύρμηξ ἑωρακὼς, τὸν τοῦ ἰξδι
πόδα ἔδακεν. ὁ δὲ, ἀλγήσας, τοὶς
τακαλάμοις ἔρριψε, καὶ τὴν πεῖσρά
ρὰν αὐτίκα φύγειν ἐποίησεν.

Ἐπιμύθιον.

ὁ μῦθος δηλοῖ, ὅτι δεῖ τοὶς εὐερ-
γέταις χάριν ἀποδιδόναι.

THE BAT, THE THORN, AND THE GULL
(Folios 24r–25v)

The bat, the thorn, and the gull decided to go into business together. So, the bat borrowed some money, the thorn bought some fabric, and the gull gathered together some copper. Then they set sail to sell their goods in a foreign port. However, while they were at sea, a violent storm arose and wrecked their ship. It was a total loss, but no lives were lost and all the ship's passengers managed to return safely to shore. Since that time, the gull patrols the waters along the coast, waiting to see if his copper will wash up on the shore. Fearful of his creditors, the bat remains concealed during the day, coming out only at night. As for the thorn, he hides in the bushes, grabbing at the clothes of all who pass by, to see if he can recover some of his lost cloth.

The moral of this fable is: First losses, like first loves, can exert a powerful influence upon the course of our lives.

f. 24r

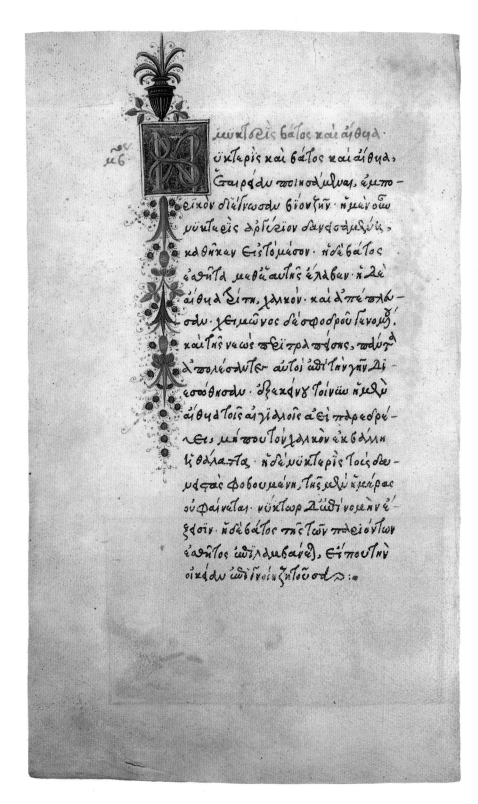

νυκτερὶς βάτος καὶ αἴθυα·
νυκτερὶς καὶ βάτος καὶ αἴθυα,
ἕταιράδν ποινοδέμναν, ἐμπο-
ρείαν διέγνωσαν βίον ζῆν ἡμερῶν
νυκταεὶς ἀργύριον δανεισαμέναι
κάθηκαν εἰς τὸ μέσον· ἡ δὲ βάτος
ἑαυτῆς μεθ᾿ αὑτῆς ἔλαβεν· ἡ δὲ
αἴθυα ἔιτη, χαλκόν· καὶ ἀπέπλε-
οσαν· χειμῶνος δὲ σφοδροῦ γενομένη,
καὶ τῆς νεὼς περιτραπείσης, πάντα
ἀπολέσαντες αὐτοὶ εἰσι τὴν γῆν δι-
εσώθησαν· ἡ βακάνε τοίνυν ἡμέ[ρ]
αἴθυα τοῖς αἰγιαλοῖς αἰεὶ παρεδρε-
ει μή που τὸν χαλκὸν ἐκβάλη
ἡ θάλαττα· ἡ δὲ νύκτερὶς τοῖς δα-
νεισταῖς φοβουμένη, τῆς μὲν ἡμέρας
οὐ φαίνεται· νύκτωρ δὲ εἰς νομὴν ἐ-
ξεισιν· ἡ δὲ βάτος τῆς τῶν πλειόντων
ἑαυτῆς εἰ περιλαμβάνει· Εἴ που τὴν
οἰκείαν εἰ εἴποι τις ζητοῦσα·

οὗτός ἐστιν ὃν ἀπώλεσαν κρεῖ\overline{το} · τοῦ
δὲ μὴ τὸ ζῆν εἶναι φαμ\overline{ψ}γ, αὖθις
καταβὰς ἀργύρων ἀνεκομί\overline{ζ} · τοῦ
δὲ, μὴ δὰ τὸ ζῆν εἶναι τὸν οἰκεῖον ἀ-
πούλος, ἐκ δ᾽ τοῦ καταβὰς ἐκεῖνον
τὸν οἶκ\overline{ον} ἀνήνεικα · τοῦ δὲ, τὸ ζῆν
ἀληθῶς εἶναι τοῦ ἀπολωλότα φα-
μένου, ὅμως ἀποδιδάμενος,
αὐτοῦ τὴν δικαιοσύνην, πᾶς
αὐτῷ ἐδωρήσατο · ὁ δὲ, παραγενό-
μενος, παρ᾽ τοῖς ἑταίροις τὰ οἰκ\overline{μ}-
βεδύτα, διεξεληλύθει · ὧν εἷς τις
τὰ τοῦ διαπράξασθαι ἐβουλόατ-
το · καὶ παρὰ τὸν ποταμὸν ὁ τ\overline{κα}ών,
καὶ τὴν οἰκείαν ἀξίνην ὃ ξεπῖτ\overline{κα}-
δὼ ἀφὰς εἰς τὸ ῥεῦμα, κλαίων
ἐκάθητο · ἐπιφανὴς οὖν ὁ ἑρμῆς
κἀκεῖνα, καὶ τὰν αἰτίαν μαθ\overline{ων}
τοῦ θρήνου, καταβὰς ὁμοίως χρυσῆν
ἀξίνην ἐξήνεγκεν · καὶ ἤρετο εἰ

THE DONKEY AND THE GARDENER

(Folios 25v–26r)

A donkey was being overworked by a gardener, and he felt very unhappy with his lot. Although he labored long and hard, the donkey was given next to nothing to eat. At last, he called upon Zeus to free him from his current master, and to find him a better one. The god heard his prayer and arranged matters so that the donkey was sold to a potter. But the donkey wasn't happy with this master either, for he had to carry heavy loads of clay and pottery. Once again, he called upon Zeus for a change of masters, and he received one—only this time he was sold to a dealer in animal hides. From the donkey's vantage point, this change was worse than all his previous situations. When he saw the nature of his new master's business, the donkey cried out: "Oh, woe is me, I should have stayed where I was in the beginning, for now I am in mortal danger of losing my skin."

The moral of this fable is: Servants rarely miss their first master as much as when they encounter those who come after him.

f. 25v

68

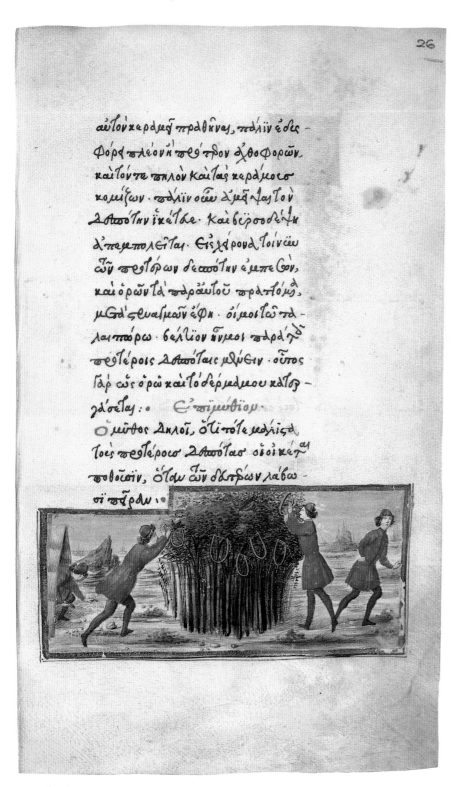

αὐτὸν καρδίαϛ πράθκναϳ, πάλιν ἔδεϲ -
φορᾳ πλέον ἢ πεϲ τρον ἀχθοφορῶν.
καὶ τόν τε πηλὸν καὶ τὰϛ κεράμοϲ
κομίζων · πάλιν οὗ̈ω ἀμα̣ϳαϳ τὸν
ἀπο̇ την ἵκελε · καὶ δεϊροσδέϳτι
ἀπεμπολεῖται · εἰς χάρουϳ τοὶνῶ
ὧ πεϲτρων δεατίην ἐμπεϲὸν,
καὶ ὁρῶν τὰ πράῳτοῦ πρατόμηϳ
μεϲα ̔ εναϳμαῶν ἔφη · οἴμοϊ τᾶϳ τά -
λαιπῶρω · βελτίων ᾖμοϊ πάρᾳ δ̇
πεϲτέροϊϲ ἀπο̇ταιϲ μϧύϬιν · οὗτος
ϳάρ ὡϲ ὁρῶ καὶ τό δέρμεϊμου κάτϳ
ϳλοϲεϳαϳ · ℰ ͞πιμύϬιον ·
ὁ μῦθος δηλοῖ, ὅτι πόλϊ μάλϳϲα
τοἰϲ πεϲτέροϊϲ ἀπο̇ταϳ οὐ οἵ κετ ̄
πολοῦϲιν, ὅτῳ ὧ ϕλϳϕῶν λάβω -
σι πάϳραν ·

THE BIRD CATCHER AND THE CRESTED LARK
(Folios 26r–26v)

A bird catcher went into the forest and began to set up his snares. From his perch high up in a tree, a crested lark noticed all the activity below and asked the bird catcher what he was doing. The bird catcher responded that he was laying out the boundaries of a new town. When he had finished, the man went away and hid himself behind some nearby bushes. The lark, taking the bird catcher at his word, flew down to investigate and found himself caught in one of the snares. As the bird catcher came running back, the lark said to him: "Excuse me, sir, but if this is the sort of city you're planning, I don't think you'll find too many people willing to live here."

The moral of this fable is: People will not want to live in cities whose rulers make life there unlivable.

HERMES AND THE TRAVELER
(Folios 26v–27r)

A traveler, who had to take a long trip, made a vow before setting out. He vowed that, if he were to find anything of value during his journey, he would offer up half of it to the god Hermes. As he walked along, he came upon a sack. Thinking it might be full of gold, he picked it up but, upon opening it, he found it contained only dates and almonds. He ate them all, one by one, carefully preserving the pits from the dates and the shells of the almonds. Placing these on a makeshift altar, the man knelt down and prayed: "Oh, Hermes, as I promised when I made my vow, here is half of what I found on my voyage."

The moral of this fable is: Thus it is with misers—even their offerings to the gods consist of only pits and shells.

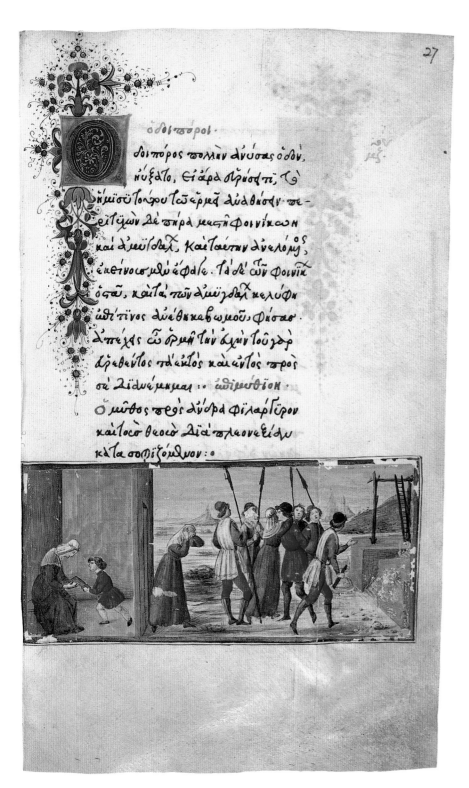

ὁδοιπόρος·

δοιπόρος πολλὴν ἀνύσας ὁδὺ,
ηὔξατο, εἰ ἅρα ὀρύση τι, τὸ
ημισυ τοῦ πυ[ρ]οῦ θεᾶ ἀναθήσειν· πε-
εἶ τ[ι] χὼν δὲ πήρα μεστῆ φοινίκων
καὶ ἀμειδάλων, καὶ τα[ῦ]την ἀνελόμε[ν]ος,
ἐκεῖνος μὲν ἔφαγε· τὰ δὲ τῶν φοινίκ[ων]
ὀστᾶ, καὶ τὰ τῶν ἀμιγδαλῶν κελύφη
ωδὶ τινος ἀνάθηκαβωμοῦ, φήσας·
ἀπέχεις ὦ ὀρμῆ τὴν ἀμὴν τοῦ γὰρ
ἀραθέντος τά αὐτὸς καὶ αὐτὸς πρὸς
σὲ ἀιδυνίμε κελαι :· ωδιρωθίοη
ὁ μῦθος πρὸς ἀνδρα φιλάργυρον
καὶ το σὸ θεοσὸ διὰ πλεονεξίαν
κατα σοφιζόμενον :·

f. 27r

THE THIEVING CHILD AND HIS MOTHER
(*Folios 27r–28r*)

A child stole some books from one of his schoolmates and brought them home to his mother. Instead of reprimanding him, she sold them. Later on, he stole someone's clothes and brought them home. Again, his mother sold the stolen goods. As the child grew older, his thefts became more frequent and began to involve items of great value. Then, one day, he was caught red-handed. The policemen tied his hands behind his back and marched him off to jail. His mother saw them taking her son away and began to weep hysterically. Her son called to her, saying that he had something that he wanted to whisper in her ear. As she leaned her head close to him, he took a great bite and ripped off her ear. She fell to the ground, screaming: "Not only do you commit crimes against the law, but also against nature!'' Her son replied: "If you had given me a good beating when I committed my first theft, I wouldn't be on my way to the gallows now.''

The moral of this fable is: Spare the rod and lose the child.

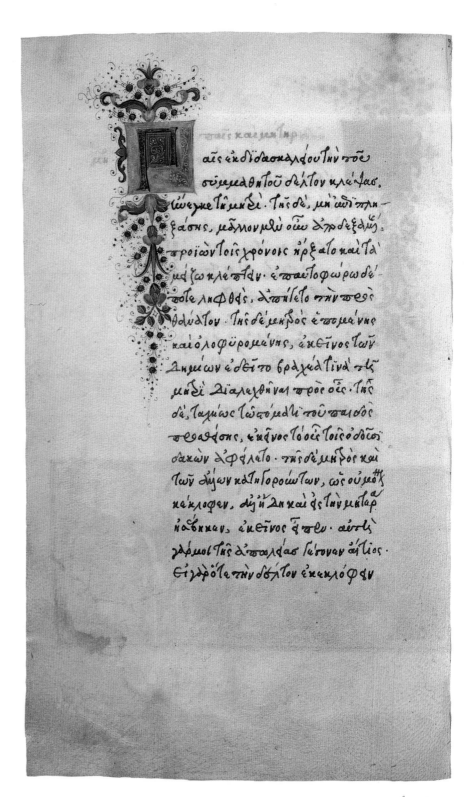

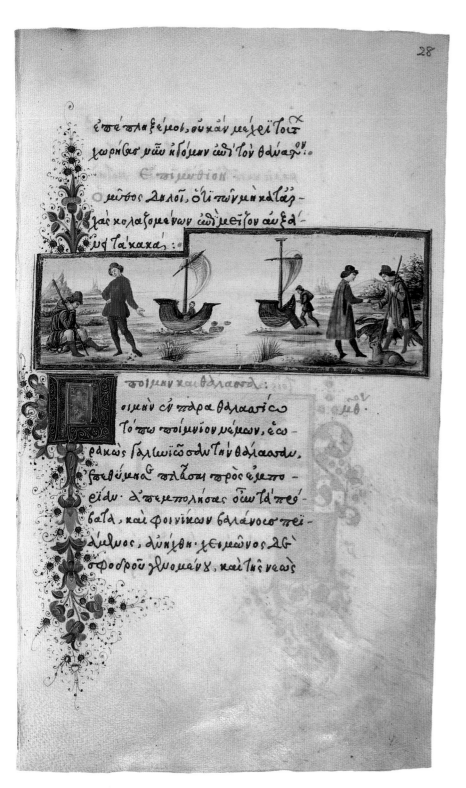

f. 28r

THE SHEPHERD AND THE SEA
(Folios 28r–28v)

One day, a shepherd was grazing his
flock along the seashore. Seeing how
calm and inviting the ocean appeared,
he thought what a good idea it would
be to travel across the sea and make his
fortune in foreign lands. So, he sold his
sheep, bought a supply of dates to sell
abroad, and set sail. But in the midst of
the voyage a terrible storm arose and his
ship was tossed about so violently that
it was in danger of sinking. To save himself, the shepherd threw his cargo over-
board. Thus lightened, the ship was able
to return safely to port. When he was
back on dry land again, the shepherd
happened to meet a man who remarked
to him how calm and placid the ocean
seemed that day. The would-be sailor
replied: "Don't be fooled, it's just
hungry for more dates—it always quiets
down when it wants another helping."

The moral of this fable is: Even accidents
can teach us valuable lessons.

THE POMEGRANATE, THE APPLE, AND THE OLIVE TREES, AND THE THORNBUSH

(Folios 28v–29r)

The pomegranate, the apple, and the olive trees were arguing about which one of them produced the most delicious fruit. As the discussion became more heated, a nearby thornbush–overhearing the argument–piped up: "Let's all be friends and stop this bickering."

The moral of this fable is: So, too, in political life, it is sometimes the lower orders who bring the rulers to their senses.

f. 28v

29

THE MOLE AND HIS MOTHER
(*Folios 29r–29v*)

One day, a baby mole (and you will
recall that all moles are blind), told his
mother that he could see quite clearly.
To prove to him that he was wrong, his
mother pushed a grain of incense beneath
his nose and asked him to identify it.
"It's a pebble," the baby mole replied.
"My poor child," said his mother, "not
only are you blind, but you also seem to
have no sense of smell."

The moral of this fable is: So, too, with
the boastful who claim that they possess
all sorts of abilities, and then are shown
to lack even the most rudimentary ones.

THE WASPS, THE PARTRIDGES, AND THE FARMER

(Folios 29v–30r)

The wasps and the partridges, consumed by a fearful thirst, begged a farmer to give them some water. In return, they promised to help him with some of his tasks. The partridges said that they would help him dig around his vines so that his grapes would grow better, and the wasps offered to help defend him by warding off thieves with their sting. The farmer responded in this manner: "I have two oxen who do all sorts of work for me without asking for anything in return. If I reward any animals for services rendered, it will be they, and not you."

The moral of this fable is: Desperate men will promise anything to have their needs fulfilled, but the results are often negative.

ὁ δὲ ἑωρ[ός] ἔφη. ἀλλέμοι[ς] ἀ-
οἰδιὸ βοὰν· οἱ μὴ δὲν ἐπαρΐελ-
λόμενοι σοῦ ἢ σοιόσοῦ. ἀμει-
μονοῦν ἀτὶν ἐκἀνοις δῦναι ἤ πρ
ἡμῖν :⁓ τελευ(τ)ίον.
ὁ μῦθος πρὸς ἀνδρασ δηλὰς, ὡ -
φηεῖν μὲν ἐπαρΐελομθύοσο. βλα-
σσόνΐας δὲ μελδἀλα ·⁓

Τάως καὶ κολοιος ·
ἀν ὀρνίθων βουλομᾶνων σοι-
ῆ σι ὁδοιλέα, Τάως ἑαυτὸν
ἠ εἴσ διὰ Ἰοκάλος χειροτονῖν.
αἱ ρουμᾶνων δε Ἰοῖπ σάνΐων,
κολοιος ὑσολαβὼν ἔφη. ἀλλὰ
σοῦ ὁδοιλόον(τ)ος ἀετὸς ἡμᾶς κζ̅ -

THE PEACOCK AND THE
JACKDAW
(*Folios 30r–30v*)

The birds were discussing the election of
their king. The peacock said that he
should be king because of his great beauty.
The other birds were in general agree-
ment with this view, and were about to
name the peacock king, when suddenly
the jackdaw asked: "But sir, if you were
king and we should be attacked by an
eagle, just what sort of help might we
expect from you?"

The moral of this fable is: One should
respect those who are always concerned
about the future and what it might hold
in store.

THE WILD BOAR AND THE FOX

(Folios 30v–31r)

One day, as a wild boar was sharpening his tusks, a fox came along and asked him why he was preparing for a fight when there seemed to be no apparent danger in the vicinity. The boar replied: "For a very good reason, I assure you—when trouble comes knocking I want to be ready for it, and I won't have time to sharpen my tusks then."

The moral of this fable is: Be prepared—don't wait until danger appears on your doorstep.

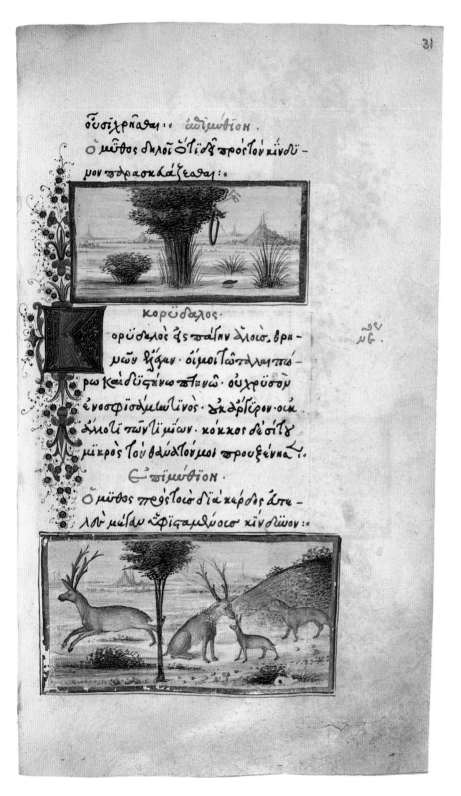

f. 31r

THE CRESTED LARK
(*Folio 31r*)

A crested lark found himself caught in a trap. In despair, he cried out: "Oh, I am such a poor, unfortunate bird! I never stole anything from anyone, neither gold, nor silver, nor anything of the slightest value. And now, just taking one tiny piece of grain has ended my life."

The moral of this fable is: There are those who are willing to risk their very lives for trifles.

THE FAWN AND THE DEER
(*Folios 31r–31v*)

One day, a fawn said to his father: "Father, you are bigger and faster than any dog, and you have those great big horns with which to defend yourself. Why is it then, that you always flee whenever dogs chase after you?" His father replied, with a smile: "All that you say is true, my child, but whenever I hear a dog bark, reason forsakes me and all I can think of is running away."

The moral of this fable is: Size, strength, and speed are of no value to a faint heart.

THE HARES AND THE FROGS
(*Folios 31v–32v*)

At a meeting one day, the hares were
bemoaning their fate—doomed to lead
short and fearful lives as the natural prey
of men, dogs, eagles, and any number of
other animals. After much discussion,
they decided to end it all, en masse,
rather than continue to tolerate such
a miserable condition. Accordingly, they
marched off toward a nearby pond, intent
upon drowning themselves. The pond
was the home of a great number of frogs
who were huddled at its edge just then.
When they heard the loud commotion
being made by all the hares as they
trooped along toward their watery grave,
the frogs became frightened and leaped,

ἑαυτῶν πρὸς ἀλλήλοις ἀπεκλαί-
οντο βίον, ὡς ἐπισφαλὴς ἦν καὶ δε-
λίας πλέως· καὶ γὰρ καὶ ἀνθρώπων,
καὶ κυνῶν, καὶ ἀετῶν, καὶ ἄλλων
πολλῶν ἀναλίσκονται· βέλτιον οὖν
εἶναι θανεῖν ἅπαξ, ἢ διὰ βίου τρέ-
μειν. τοῦτο τοίνυν κυρώσαντες, ὥρ-
μησαν κατὰ ταὐτὸν εἰς τὴν λίμνην,
ὡς εἰς αὐτὴν ἐμπεσούμενοι καὶ ἀπο-
πνιγησόμενοι· τῶν δὲ καθημένων
κύκλῳ τῆς λίμνης βατράχων, ὡς
τὸν τοῦ δρόμου κτύπον ᾔσθοντο, δι-
θέως εἰς αὐτὴν εἰσπηδησάντων,
ταῦτα λαγωός τις ἀγχινούστερος ἦναι
δοκῶν τῶν ἄλλων, ἔφη· στῆτε ἑται-
ροι· μηδὲν δεινὸν ἡμᾶς αὐτοὺς δι-
απράξασθε· ἤδη γὰρ ὁρᾶτε καὶ ἡ-
μῶν ἕτερα ζῶα δειλότερα.

Ἐπιμύθιον·

Ὁ μῦθος δηλοῖ, ὅτι οἱ δῦστυχοῦντες

---

all together, into the pond. Seeing this,
one of the hares (who was a trifle
smarter than the others) said to his
fellow animals: "Just a moment, friends,
let's reconsider our intention, for–as
you can see–there are creatures who are
afraid of us!"

The moral of this fable is: It may take
the unhappiness of others to put one's
own misfortunes in perspective.

f. 32r

THE DONKEY WHO ENVIED
THE HORSE'S LIFE
(Folios 32v–33r)

A donkey was envious of a horse who
always seemed to be well-fed and well-
groomed. The donkey found this an
unhappy contrast with the minimal
amount of food that he received, and
the hard work he was expected to do.
But soon after he had these thoughts,
war was declared. The horse went to war,
carrying a fully armed man on his back.
His master rode him into the midst of
battle, driving him this way and that.
Finally, the horse was felled by an
enemy's blow and died. Hearing of the
horse's fate, the donkey saw things
differently, and envy gave way to pity.

The moral of this fable is: Spare yourself
the burden of envying the rich and powerful, since they, too, have their sorrows.

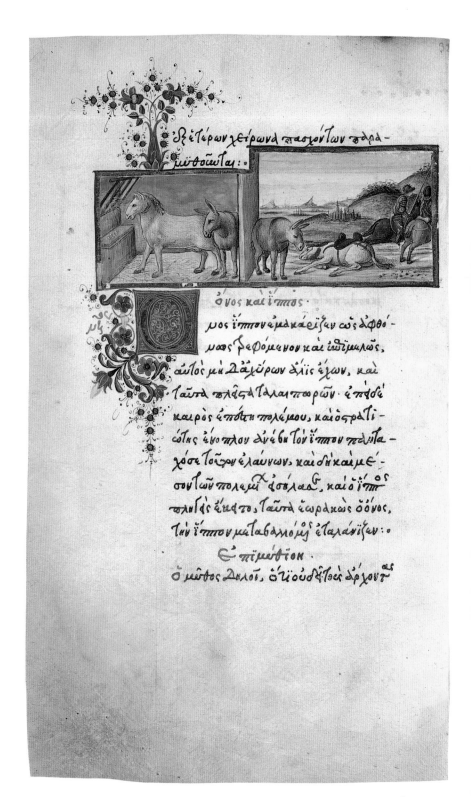

f. 32v

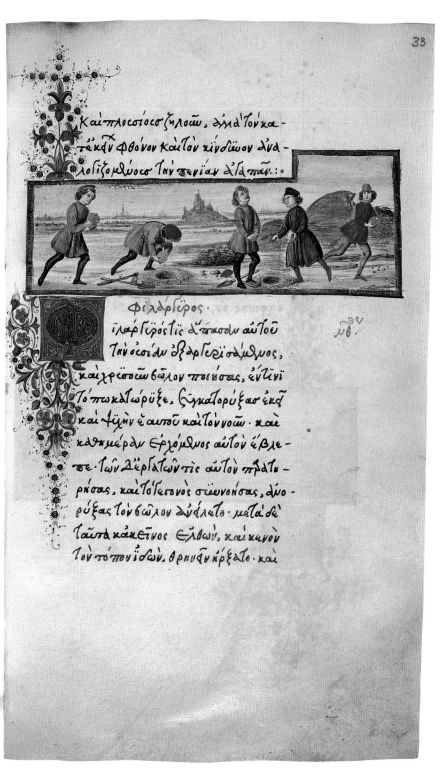

33

Καὶ πλουσίους ζηλοῖ, ἀλλὰ τοῦ κα-
τὲκὰν φθόνον καὶ τὸν κίνδυνον ἀνα-
λογίζομενος τὴν πενίαν ἀγαπᾷ·:–

Φιλάργυρος·
ὶλάργυρός τις ἅπασαν αὐτοῦ
τὴν οὐσίαν ἐξαργυρισάμενος,
καὶ χρυσοῦν βῶλον ποιήσας, ἐν τινι
τόπω κατώρυξε. Ξυνατορύξας ἐκεῖ
καὶ τὴν ἑαυτοῦ καὶ τὸν νοῦν. καὶ
καθημέραν ἐρχόμενος αὐτὸν ἔβλε-
πε· τῶν δ' ἐργατῶν τις αὐτὸν πρὰτ-
ρήσας, καὶ τὸ γεγονὸς σὺννοήσας, ἀνο-
ρύξας τὸν βῶλον ἀφείλετο· μετὰ δὲ
ταῦτα κἀκεῖνος ἐλθὼν, καὶ κενὸν
τὸν τόπον ἰδὼν, θρηνῶν ἤρξατο. καὶ

THE MISER
(Folios 33r–33v)

There once was a miser who sold all his possessions and melted down the gold he received in return for them into a single ingot. This he buried in a secret hiding place and, without realizing it, he also left his heart and soul there. Every day, without fail, he would visit the spot where the gold was buried and gaze fondly upon his treasure. One day, however, he was observed doing this and, after he had left, the observer dug up the ingot and ran off with it. When the miser came back the next day and found his gold gone he began to wail and tear his hair in a frenzy of despair over his loss. A passerby came over to find out what was wrong and, after being told the miser's story, said: "You really should not be so upset, old friend. You may have thought you possessed all this gold, but—in reality—you had nothing. Take a large rock and put it in the hole where you had hidden the ingot. You will find that it serves the same purpose, for you made no use of the gold when it was there anyway."

The moral of this fable is: Riches amount to nothing if one cannot enjoy them.

THE GEESE AND THE CRANES

(Folios 33v–34r)

A flock of geese and some cranes were
searching for food in a small valley.
Suddenly, hunters appeared; the agile
cranes flew off, but the heavy geese,
unable to move quickly because of their
weight, were all captured and killed.

The moral of this fable is: So, too, with
men–when a city is victimized by war
or revolution, the poor (having little to
carry or leave behind) are free to flee
to another country and thus save themselves. But the rich are impeded by the
bulk of their possessions, and must often
remain, to either perish or be enslaved.

f. 33v

34

THE TORTOISE AND THE EAGLE
(*Folios 34r–34v*)

A tortoise begged an eagle to teach him how to fly. The eagle replied that this really was impossible, since the tortoise was not designed for flight. But the tortoise refused to take no for an answer, and continued to plead with the eagle. Finally, the bird gave in and, grasping the tortoise in his talons, flew off with him. When they were high up in the sky, the eagle released the tortoise, who plummeted to the ground with a thud, and died.

The moral of this fable is: In trying to imitate others, with whom one has nothing in common, one can do oneself great harm.

f. 34r

THE FLEA AND THE MAN
(Folios 34v–35r)

One day, a flea was pestering a man relentlessly. Finally, the man caught hold of it and said: "Just who do you think you are, chewing on every part of my body and causing me such pain and injury?" The flea responded: "I am a flea, and that's what fleas do. Please don't kill me, I'm really not that much of a bother." The man laughed scornfully at this and said: "I *am* going to kill you, because whatever the evil, great or small, it must be eliminated."

The moral of this fable is: One should show no pity toward an evildoer, whether great or small.

35

THE BLIND DOE
(Folios 35r–35v)

There was a doe who had lost the sight in one of her eyes. She went down to the seashore one day to feed, keeping her good eye toward the land in case there might be any hunters in the vicinity. Her blind eye faced the ocean, from which she expected no danger. But a boat passed by, and when the sailors saw the doe, they brought their vessel in close to shore and killed her. As she was breathing her last, she said to herself: "Oh, what a sad fool I am—my good eye looked for trouble on land where there is always danger for me, so I didn't look toward the sea, from which I thought no harm could come. But it is the sea that has brought me death."

The moral of this fable is: So, too, with men—sometimes we look for danger where there is only peace and quiet, and sometimes where we look for peace and quiet, we find danger.

THE DOE AND THE LION
(Folio 35v)

Desperate to escape from a pack of
hunters who were chasing her, a doe
looked about frantically and spied a cave
with a lion resting at the entrance.
Without thinking, she leaped over him
and disappeared inside. The lion promptly
followed her into the cave and attacked
her. As the lion was about to kill her,
the doe cried out: "How ill-fated I am—
to escape my human enemies, only to be
slaughtered by a ferocious animal."

The moral of this fable is: So, too,
among men—we sometimes find our-
selves facing a greater danger, due to
our fear of a lesser one.

THE DOE AND THE VINES
(Folios 35v–36r)

A doe, pursued by hunters, hid herself in
a vineyard. When the hunters passed by,
she assumed that she had fooled them
completely, and so she began to munch
on the vine leaves. Foolishly, she failed
to notice that her munching made the
vines sway, and this was her undoing.
Doubling back to look for her, the
hunters saw the movement of the vines
and caught the doe. At the point of
death, the doe groaned: "It's all my own
fault, for I should not have done harm
to that which had saved me."

f. 35v

f. 36r

The moral of this fable is: People who injure those who have helped them will be punished by the gods.

THE DONKEY, THE ROOSTER, AND THE LION
(Folios 36r–36v)

A rooster and a donkey were grazing together one day. Suddenly, along came a hungry lion, who made a menacing move toward the donkey. The rooster cried out and the lion fled, for—as everyone knows—a lion is afraid of the sound of a rooster's crowing. The donkey, seeing the lion flee, was struck by the notion that the lion must be afraid of *him*. So, he foolishly gave chase. He pursued the lion for quite some distance, leaving the rooster far behind. When the sound of the rooster's crowing could no longer be heard, the lion stopped running, turned around, and pounced on the donkey. As he lay dying, the donkey said: "What a sad fool am I! I am no predator, what on earth ever made me think I could become one?"

The moral of this fable is: Beware of attacking an enemy who only appears weak, or you may wind up as dinner for one.

89

THE GARDENER AND THE DOG
(*Folio 36v*)

[*Miniature only. The Greek text is missing.*]

[The text for this fable tells the story of a dog who fell into a well. When the gardener descended into the depths to haul him out, the dog—in his fear and confusion—misunderstood the gardener's intentions, and bit him. The gardener said: "This is what I deserve. Why did I try to rescue you when it was your own action that brought you into harm's way in the first place?"]

f. 36v

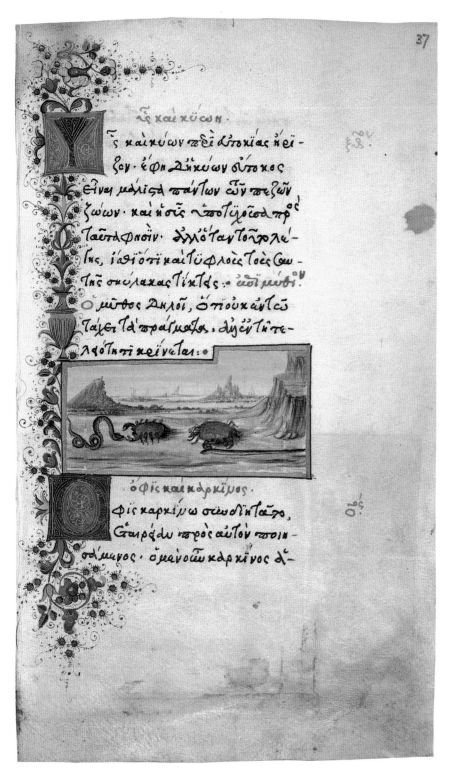

THE SOW AND THE DOG
(*Folio 37r*)

[*Greek text only. The minature is missing.*]

A sow and a dog were arguing over which of them produced a litter with greater ease. The dog alleged that, of all four-legged animals, she had the shortest period of pregnancy. "No wonder, then," sniffed the sow in reply, "that all your pups are born blind."

The moral of this fable is: One should judge a deed not by the speed with which it is done, but by the quality of the finished product.

THE SNAKE AND THE CRAB
(*Folios 37r–37v*)

A snake and a crab were dwelling, rather uneasily, close together. The crab was very polite to the snake, but the snake was all surliness and hostility. The crab urged the snake to change his ways and to show the same consideration toward him that he showed toward the reptile. But the snake would not listen and persisted in his bad behavior. This made the crab so angry that, one day, when he found the snake asleep, he seized him by the throat and killed him. Seeing the snake stretched out in death, the crab said: "Well, friend, it's a bit late to straighten yourself out at this point. You should have heeded my advice to mend your ways while you were alive— it's not much use now."

The moral of this fable is: So, too, with men who are nasty to their friends and neighbors during their lifetimes but, after death, leave something good behind— even if it's only their absence.

THE SHEPHERD AND THE WOLF
(Folios 37v–38r)

A shepherd found a newborn wolf cub in the hills and brought the little wolf home to be raised among his dogs. Once the wolf cub was fully grown, he would often join the dogs when they went off to chase another, sheep-stealing wolf. Sometimes, the dogs would give up, but the wolf would continue the chase and— when he caught up with his fellow wolf— he would share in the prey instead of attacking the thief. On other occasions, the wolf would kill a sheep on the sly and share it with the dogs. In time, however, when the shepherd realized what was happening, he killed the wolf and hung him from a tree as an example.

The moral of this fable is: Once a wolf, always a wolf.

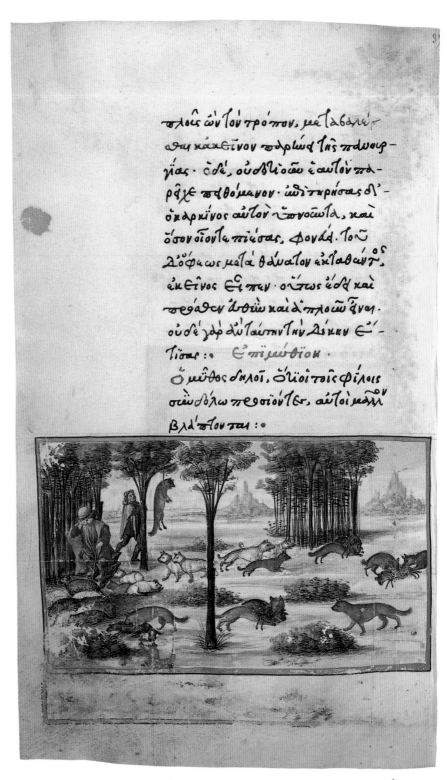

f. 37v

ποιμὴν καὶ λύκος

Οἱ μὴν νεογνὸν λύκου σκύμνον
εὑρὼν καὶ ἀναλεγόμενος, σὺν
τοῖς κυσὶν ἔτρεφεν· ἐπειδὴ ξιξ,
εἰ ποτε λύκος πρόβατον ἥρπαζε,
μετὰ τῶν κυνῶν καὶ αὐτὸς ἐδίω-
κε. τῶν δὲ κυνῶν ἔσθ' ὅτε μὴ δυνα-
μένων καταλαβεῖν τὸν λύκον, καὶ
διὰ τοῦτο ἀποστραφόντων, ἐκεῖνος
ἀκολουθῶν, μέχρις ἂν τοῦ ζῴου κατα-
λαβὼν οἷα δὴ λύκος οὗ μετάσχοι
τῆς θοίρας. εἶτα ὑπέστρεφεν· εἰ
δὲ μὴ λύκος ἔξωθεν ἁρπάσαι τι
πρόβατον, αὐτὸς λάθρα θύων, δ—
μετὰ τοῖς κυσὶν ἐθοινᾶτο. ἕως ὁ ποιμὴν στοχασάμενος, καὶ συνεὶς τὸ
δρώμενον, ἐπὶ δένδρου αὐτὸν ἀ-
ναρτήσας διώλεσεν :· ὁ μῦθι
ὁ μῦθος δηλοῖ, ὅτι ἡ φύσις πο-
νηρὰ χρηστὸν ἦθος οὐ τρέφει :·

THE LION, THE WOLF, AND THE FOX
(Folios 38r–39r)

A lion, aged and infirm, lay dying in his cave. All the animals came to pay their respects, except the fox. The wolf, sensing that there might be something to gain from this situation, began denigrating the fox to the lion. Said the wolf: "He has no respect for you, the king of beasts, that's why he hasn't come to see you." While he was speaking, however, the fox arrived and overheard the wolf's words. At the sight of the fox, the lion roared his disapproval, but the fox asked for the opportunity to defend himself. "Who," he began, "of all the animals assembled here, has been as much use to you as I? I, who have searched everywhere on your behalf for a cure, and have actually found one." The lion asked the fox what this cure was. "First, you skin a wolf alive," the fox answered, "and then you cover yourself with the skin while it is still warm." When the wolf heard this prescription, he began to quiver and quake. Noting the wolf's reaction, the fox said with a smile: "One shouldn't encourage cruelty in a master, but kindness instead."

The moral of this fable is: Be careful about setting a trap for someone else—you may fall into it yourself.

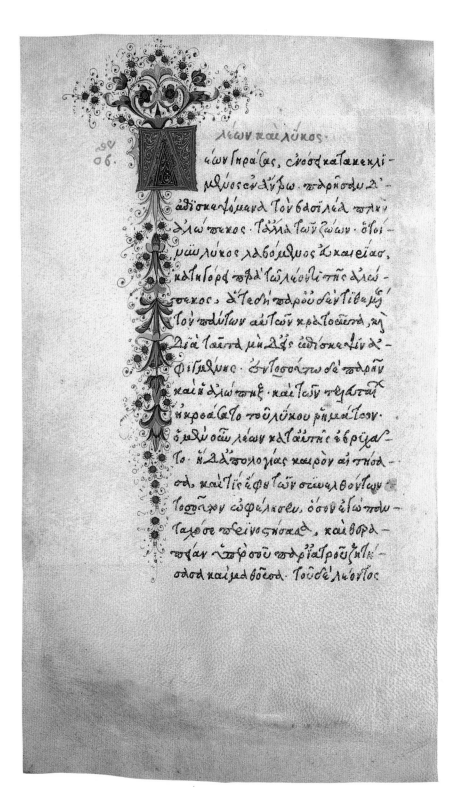

f. 39r

THE WOMAN AND THE DRUNKARD
(Folios 39r–40r)

A woman had the misfortune to be married to a drunkard. At last, she decided to try to trick him into sobriety. Waiting until late one night, when her husband had drunk himself into a stupor, she hoisted him onto her shoulders and carried him off to the cemetery, where she deposited him in a mausoleum. She then returned home. When it seemed that sufficient time had passed for her husband to have sobered up, she returned to the cemetery and knocked on the door of the mausoleum. "Who's that knocking?" asked her husband. "I have come to feed the dead," said the wife, disguising her voice. Came the reply: "Forget about the food, I need a drink." Hearing this, the woman lost heart and cried out: "Oh, this is the last straw! My ruse has had no effect upon you, has it, husband? Instead, it has shown me that drunkenness is imbued in your very soul."

The moral of this fable is: With some people, vice is ingrained.

λάξαι θέλοισ᾽. τοιοῦ δὲ τίσοφί[ζε]· κε-
καρωμένου οὐ γὰρ αὐτὸν ἀπὸ τῆς μέθης
ὑδραγωγήσασ, καὶ νεκροῦ δίκην
ἀναισθητοῦντα, ἐπ᾽ ὤμων ἄρασ
ἐπὶ τόπον ὕδωριον ἀπενεγκοῦσα
κατέθετο καὶ ἀπῆλθεν· ἰωναπ᾽ δ᾽
αὐτὸν ἤδη ἀνανήφειν ὅτε γοναωστο,
προσρίβωσα τὴν θύραν ἔκωπτε
τοῦ πολὺ δυσεῖ· ἐκείνου δὲ φηλυ-
τος τίς ὁ τὴν θύραν κόπτων, ἣ τοῦ ἃ
ἀπεκείνατο. ὁ τοῖς νεκροῖς τὰ
σιτία κομίζων, ἐγὼ παρ ᾽ ἃ κᾱ-
κεῖνος μή μοι φαίνεῖν ἀλλ᾽ τοῖ-
εῖν ὦ θειλίτισι μᾶλλον πεσούνει-
κε. λιπῷς γάρ μ᾽ε βρώσεως δι-
λὰ μὴ πότος μυημονεύων· ἤ δὲ,
τὸ ὄπωθος προλάξασ οἴμοι τοῖ δῦ-
στηνω φησῖν. οὐδὲ γὰρ οὐδὲ το-
φίος δυμένι ἄνησα. οὐ γὰρ αὐ Ἐρ
οὐ μόνον γ᾽ κ ἐπαιοδ᾽ὅσοσ. ἀλλ᾽

40

THE BOAR AND THE MOUSE
(Folio 40r)

A hungry boar was quarreling with a mouse over some food that each one said belonged to him. The mouse and the boar both had their teeth in the morsel, but the boar was dragging both food and mouse along. This was observed by some blacksmiths who laughed at the mismatched struggle. Tearfully, the mouse begged them to help him, but in response, the men just laughed even harder.

The moral of this fable is: Those who are unable to take care of their own affairs should expect nothing but scorn from others.

THE DONKEY IN THE LION'S SKIN
(Folios 40r–40v)

A donkey draped a lion's skin around his body, and this disguise was so convincing that even men fled at the sight of him. He had not secured the skin very carefully, however, and so, when a strong wind arose, the lion's skin blew away and the donkey's ruse was revealed to the whole world. When the formerly frightened men saw how they had been fooled, they ran up and began to beat the donkey. When they had finished, they harnessed him to a grindstone as his reward for impersonating the king of beasts.

The moral of this fable is: Do not try to appear to be what you are not, since you may find the punishment for such a pretense to be quite severe.

THE SPARROW
(*Folio 40v*)

One day, when all the birds and animals were making music together, a sparrow from Libya put himself forward as their leader. He tricked the land creatures into thinking he was one of them by showing that he, too, had legs.

The moral of this fable is: Those who would claim to serve two masters must be deceiving one of them.

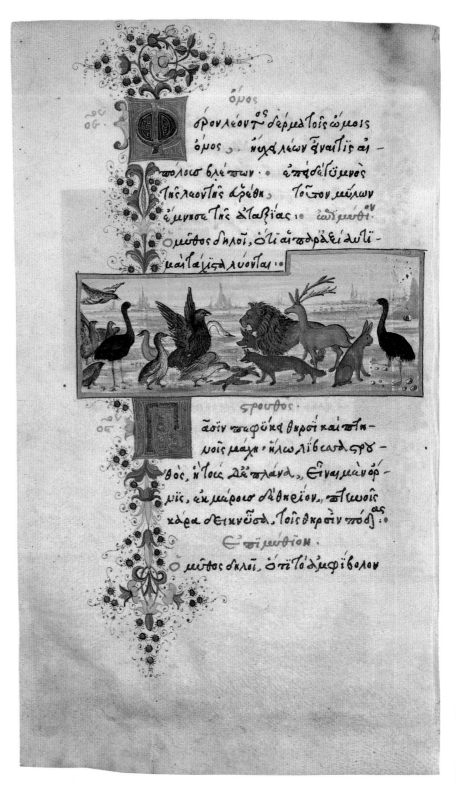

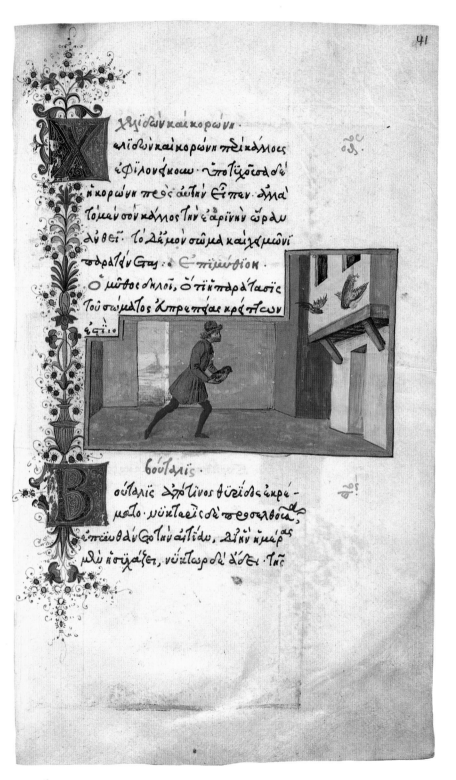

f. 41r

THE SWALLOW AND THE CROW
(*Folio 41r*)

[*Greek text only. The miniature is missing.*]

A swallow and a crow were arguing over which one was more beautiful. To the arguments of the swallow, the crow replied: "Your beauty flourishes only in spring, while I have a form adaptable to all seasons, even the coldest winter."

The moral of this fable is: It is better to have a functional body than a beautiful one.

THE NIGHTINGALE AND THE BAT
(*Folios 41r–41v*)

There was a nightingale, confined to a cage hung in a window, who would sing all night long. A bat heard the sound and flew over to the nightingale's cage. He asked the nightingale why he remained silent all day, and then burst into song at night. The nightingale answered: "For a very good reason. It was during the day that I was taken captive, and so now I am careful about making any noise in the daytime." The bat remarked: "Surely, such behavior is pointless now—you should have exercised caution earlier, before you were caught."

99

The moral of this fable is: When one has suffered a misfortune, regrets serve no useful purpose.

THE SNAILS

(Folios 41v–42r)

A little boy was frying some snails in a pan. When he heard them crackle in the oil he said: "Silly creatures, your houses are burning around you, and you sing."

The moral of this fable is: One's reaction to misfortune should be appropriate to the experience.

42

THE WOMAN AND THE SERVANTS
(*Folios 42r–42v*)

An old woman had a farm where she employed a number of young servants. She depended upon her rooster to crow very early in the morning to awaken the servants for work, but they disliked this intensely, since their sleep was interrupted at such an early hour that they were constantly tired. Eventually, the servants decided to kill the rooster, thinking that once he was gone, they wouldn't have to get up so early. This only made their situation worse, however, for the woman began to rise even earlier than the rooster had, and so–of necessity–did the servants.

The moral of this fable is: So, too, with many people–they bring trouble upon themselves by their own actions.

f. 42r

THE MAGICIAN

(Folios 42v–43r)

A female magician set up shop and began to sell good-luck charms and amulets guaranteed to ward off the wrath of the gods. Business was good and she soon prospered greatly. With prosperity, however, came notoriety, and the local priests observed her activities with displeasure. Claiming that her sale of charms and amulets amounted to heresy, they had her arrested, and—after a brief trial— she was condemned to death. Seeing the woman being led off to her execution, a passerby called out: "Some magician you are! You claimed to be able to protect others from the wrath of the gods. How can it be that you are unable to save yourself from the wrath of men?"

The moral of this fable is: Be skeptical of anyone who claims to be able to work miracles, and yet cannot manage to overcome life's ordinary crises.

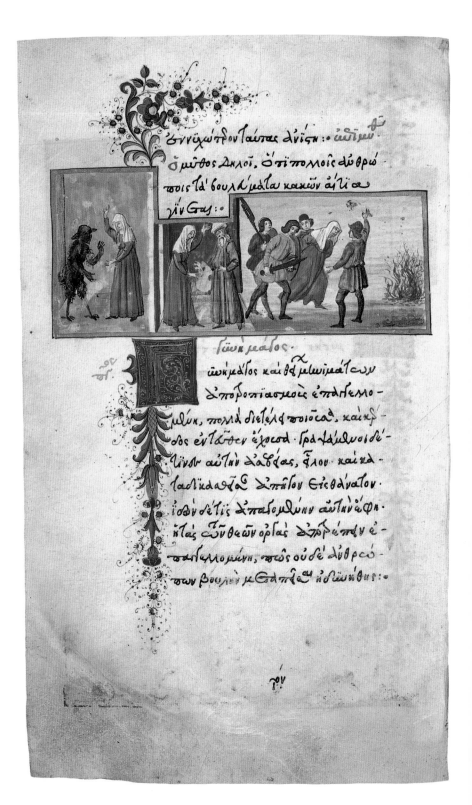

ωτμύθιον·

ὁ μῦθος δηλοῖ, ὅτι πολλοὶ μεγάλα
ἐπαγγέλλονται, μηδὲ μικρά ποιῆσαι
δυνάμενοι·∶

THE WEASEL AND THE FILE
(Folio 43r)

A weasel sneaked into a blacksmith's
shop and began to lick a file that he
found there. As he licked harder, the
edge of the file cut his tongue. His blood
began to flow freely, but he would not
stop licking. Somehow, he convinced
himself that the blood was coming from
the iron file and he licked even harder,
so that—in the end—he cut his entire
tongue off.

The moral of this fable is: Those who
insist upon confrontations with others
may sometimes find that they do themselves more harm than good.

THE FARMER AND THE GOD-DESS FORTUNE
(Folios 43r–43v)

A farmer was out digging in his fields
one day, when he unearthed a great
hoard of gold. In gratitude for his good
fortune, he made a special sacrifice each
succeeding day to the Earth Goddess,
since he assumed that it was she who
had bestowed this favor upon him.
Then, one day, the Goddess Fortune

appeared to the man and said: "Can you tell me, my good man, why you attribute your good fortune to the Earth Goddess? Don't you realize that it was I who intended that you be enriched? If, at some time in the future you should be deprived of that gold, I am sure you will not hesitate to blame me for your misfortune."

The moral of this fable is: One ought to acknowledge favors properly, and thank a benefactor accordingly.

THE TRAVELERS AND THE AXE
(*Folios 43v–44r*)

Two men were traveling along together. One of them saw an axe by the side of the road and picked it up. His companion said: "How lucky we are to have found an axe." The other man replied: "No, *we* didn't find an axe, *I* did." A few moments later, they encountered a group of men who claimed that the axe was theirs. They demanded that it be returned to them, but the man who had found it refused. As the outraged owners began to beat the traveler, he cried out to his friend: "We are lost." "Don't say *we* are

lost," came the reply, "say *I* am lost, for when you found the axe you didn't want to share it."

The moral of this fable is: Those who are not permitted to share in the good fortune of a friend will not want any part of his misfortune.

THE FROGS
(*Folios 44r–44v*)

There were two frogs who lived in the same neighborhood. One of them lived in a deep pond and the other dwelt in a little puddle alongside a road. The one who lived in the pond invited the other frog to move in with him. Together, he said, they would have a better and more secure life. But the puddle dweller refused, saying that he did not want to change the way of life to which he had become accustomed. So, one day, a chariot came racing along the road, veered off through the puddle, and crushed that frog to death.

f. 44r

The moral of this fable is: So, too, among men–those with bad habits would sometimes rather die than make any changes for the better.

THE BEEKEEPER

(*Folios 44v–45r*)

A thief stole honey and honeycombs from the hives of a beekeeper who was away on an errand. When the beekeeper returned, he saw what had happened and began checking the hives for any damage. Meanwhile, the bees came back from their own errands and, finding their precious nectar gone, began to sting the beekeeper viciously. Covering his face with his hands, he roared at them: "Stupid insects, you should be off chasing the thief instead of attacking the person who has always taken good care of you!"

The moral of this fable is: So, too, among men, who sometimes fail to realize who their real enemies are–instead, they accuse their friends of treachery.

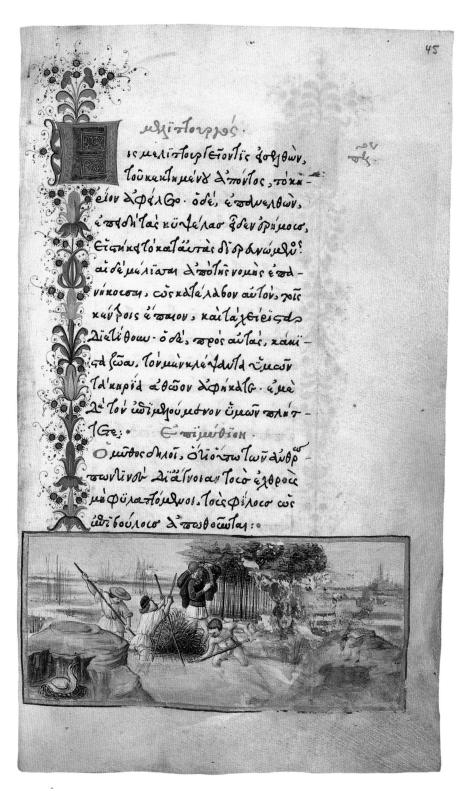

f. 45r

THE KINGFISHER
(Folios 45r–46r)

The kingfisher is a bird who likes to be alone, perching on some rocky promontory near the sea. One day, a kingfisher, searching for a nesting place, found a rock overhanging the sea and built her nest there. Then she flew off to find some food for herself and her chicks. While the bird was away, a fierce storm blew up and the sea rose and covered the nest, drowning the chicks. When the kingfisher returned and saw what had happened, she cried out: "Oh, how unfortunate I am! I have always looked upon the sea as my friend, but now I find that it can be as cruel to me as any fisherman ever was."

The moral of this fable is: So, too, among men, who sometimes concentrate upon defending themselves against their enemies, only to find that their friends are a far greater threat than any enemy ever could be.

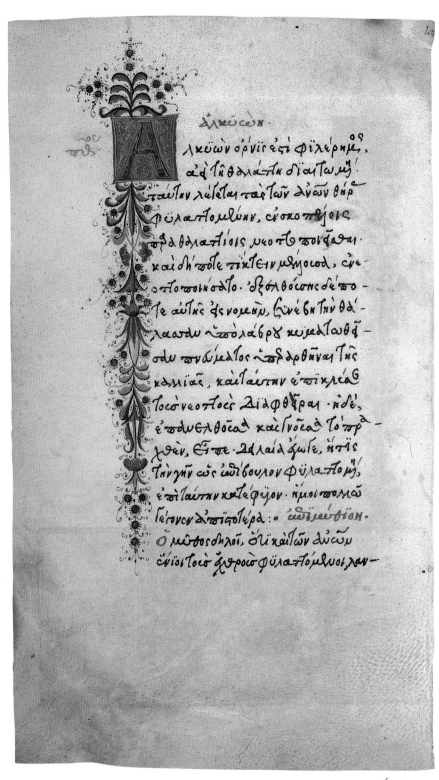

ἀλκυὼν·

Ἀλκυὼν ὄρνίς ἐςὶ φιλέρημος,
καὶ τῇ θαλάτηι διαιτωμένη·
ταύτην λέγεται τὰς τῶν ᾠῶν θήρα
φιλαρτομένων, ἐν σκοπέλοις
ἐν θαλαϋίοις νεοῠ ᾠ ποιεῖϑαι·
καὶ δῆ τῷ δε τίκτειν μήλο ϊσϑ, ἐν
τῷ ποωποιήϑατο. ἐξολοθϋϊονς δὲ τῷ
τε αὐτῆς ϊς νομεῶ, ϊνέβη τῇ θά-
λαϋαν ϊπολάβρω κεχαλαϑῷ-
ον πυϊμέϊϊος ϊϊφ δϊρθϊϊνα τῆς
κολμίας, καὶ ϊαύτην ϊποϊπλέα
τοϊὸν νεοϊϊϊς διαφθϊϊραι· ϊδέ,
ϊ πϊϊϊνϊλθόϊϊϊ καὶ τοϊϊϊ τὸ ϊπϊ-
χϊϊν, ϊϊτε διλλαιδ ϊμϊϊϊ, ϊτϊϊϊ
τὴνϊὴν ϊς ϊωϊϊβουλον φϊϊλαϊτομϊϊ,
ϊ τϊϊαύτην καϊϊϊφίλον· ἠμοϊ ποϊϊϊ
ϊϊτϊϊγϊν ϊπϊϊτϊϊϊϊϊρα :· ϊωϊϊϊϊϊϊϊον·
ὁ μϊϊϊοϊ δϊϊλοϊ, ϊτι καϊϊϊν ϊϊϊϊν
ϊνϊοϊ τοϊὸ ϊϊϊφροϊϊ φϊϊλαϊτομϊϊνοι, καν—

46

THE FISHERMAN
(Folios 46r–46v)

A fisherman was plying his trade in a river. First, he stretched his net across the water, securing it to trees on both banks. Then, attaching a stone to a rope, he began thrashing the water. The fish in the river, frightened by the turbulence thus created, tried to flee and were caught in the net. A man who lived nearby saw what was going on and reproached the fisherman for stirring up the river and, thereby, muddying his drinking water. The fisherman answered: "The price of your clear water would be my death from hunger."

The moral of this fable is: So, too, with affairs of state—demagogues don't care how much turmoil they create, as long as they can remain in power.

f. 46r

THE MONKEY AND THE DOLPHIN

(Folios 46v–47r)

When they are embarking upon a long sea voyage, many people like to bring a little dog or a monkey along to divert them. One such traveler began a sea voyage with a little monkey as his companion. As the ship was rounding a cape in Greece, a violent storm blew up and the ship capsized. Everyone aboard managed to jump into the sea before the ship sank, however, including the monkey. A passing dolphin saw the monkey and, mistaking him for a man, slid beneath him and carried him toward the shore. When they arrived at Piraeus, the port of Athens, the dolphin asked the monkey if he was an Athenian. The monkey answered that he was, and added that he came from a rather distinguished family. The dolphin then asked the monkey if he knew Piraeus well. The monkey, not knowing what it was, answered: "Oh yes, Piraeus is one of my best friends." The dolphin was so incensed by this

f. 46v

transparent lie that he dumped the monkey into the water, where the animal drowned.

The moral of this fable is: You can fool some of the dolphins some of the time, but the attempt is fraught with peril.

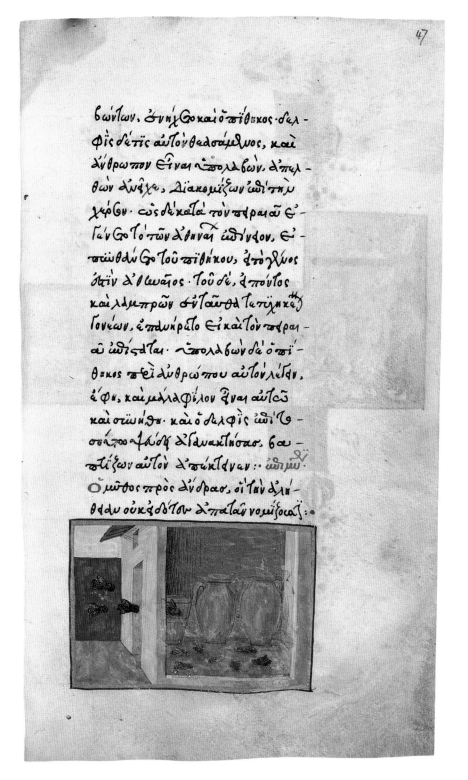

THE FLIES
(*Folios 47r–47v*)

When a jar of honey tipped over, a swarm of flies settled on the honey immediately, and began to gorge themselves. It was such a sweet feast that the flies couldn't pull themselves away. Soon, this became literally true, as their legs became stuck in the mire of spilled honey, which held them fast. The flies, despairing of ever escaping, bemoaned their fate, crying: "Oh, how unhappy we are–for a brief bout of pleasure we must now perish."

The moral of this fable is: Gluttons– heed the fate of the flies.

HERMES AND THE SCULPTOR

(*Folios 47v–48r*)

Hermes was curious about his standing among men. So, he changed into mortal form and descended to earth, where he visited the studio of a sculptor. While there, he saw a statue of Zeus and asked the sculptor the price. "One drachma," the artist answered. Hermes smiled and inquired: "How much is the statue of Hera?" The answer came back: "More expensive than that of Zeus." Then, Hermes saw a statue of himself, and presuming that he must be held in great esteem by mankind (since he was both Zeus's messenger and the god of profit), he asked how much the statue cost. The sculptor answered: "If you take the other two, you can have that one for nothing."

The moral of this fable is: Such is the fate of a vain man whose exalted opinion of himself is not shared by others.

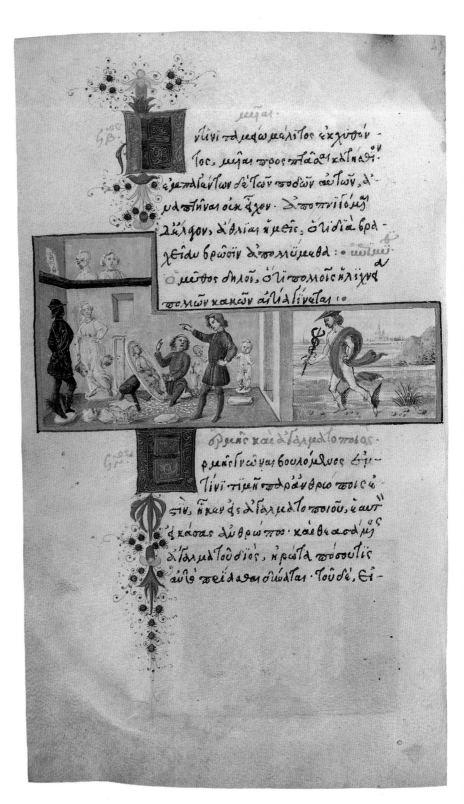

f. 47v

112

48

HERMES AND TIRESIAS
(Folios 48r–49r)

Hermes wanted to put Tiresias's soothsaying power to the test, so he stole Tiresias's oxen and then appeared to him in the guise of a traveler. In response to the theft of his animals, Tiresias went out with Hermes to perform an augury through the vehicle of a bird in flight. He asked Hermes to tell him when he saw a bird. First, Hermes saw an eagle, which flew from left to right, and he told this to Tiresias. Tiresias replied that this bird didn't count. Then the god saw a crow perch on a branch. As the bird alternately raised and lowered his eyes, Hermes told the prophet about this. Tiresias replied: "This crow swears by heaven and earth that it's in your power to have my oxen returned."

The moral of this fable is: Even if his disguise is a good one, a thief should beware of being unmasked.

κλέψας τὰς αὐτοῦ βοῦς ὃς ἀγροικίας,
ἧκεν ὡς αὐτὸν ἧς ἀγ͂ ὁμοιωθεὶς ἀν-
θρώπῳ· καὶ πρὸ αὐτῶ καταχθεὶ. Τῆς
δὲ τῶν βοῶν ἀπωλείας ἀπελθεὶ
ᾧ Ἰφευσία, ἀκεῖνος παραλαβὼν
τὸν ἑρμῆν ἐξῆλθεν, οἰωνοί τινα περὶ
τοῦ κλέπτου σκαπτόμενος· καὶ τού-
τῳ παρήγγ Δάξενατῶ, ὅντινα ἂν
τῶν ὀρνίθων θεάσηται. ὁ δὲ ἑρμῆς
τὸ μὲν πρῶτον θεασάμενος ἀετὸν
ἐξδεξιᾷ στρῶν ὑπεῖα δεξιὰ Διΐ πλα-
μένον, ἔφρα. τοῦ δὲ φησὶ δυτος
μὴ πρὸς αὐτοὺς ἀνατολῶν, ἀλλ
τῷ ῥουχορώνου ᾧ δὲ νῶ τίνος δαυδρ
καθημένην, καὶ πολὺ μὲν ἄνω βλέ-
πουσαν, πολὺ δὲ πρὸς τὴν γῆν κατα
κύπτουσαν· καὶ τῷ μὲν τῇ φράζ.
καὶ ὃς ὑπομειδιῶν εἶπαν. ἀλλ ἀπη-
γὴν κορώνη λέγεν ὑπᾶς τόν γε ὁ αἰῶνον
καὶ τὴν γῆν, ὡς ἐὰν οὐδ ἑλῃς· τὰς

ἐμὰς ἀπολήψομαι βόες :· ἐωὶ μεν
τ · ο᾽τω τῶ λόγω χρήσομ τοδαύτιι πρὸς
ἀνδρα κλέπ την :·

κυνⲉ·

χωντίς διὸ κώνας, Τοὺμ δὺ ἐ-
Ίφον θηρᾶν ἐδίδαξε, Τοὺδέ
λοιπὸν οἰκοφῦλακεῖν · καὶ δὴ ἅ ποτε
ὁ θηρλτικὸς ἡἵρδκῖι, καὶ ὁ οἰκοςρὸς
σὺ μμεῖΐεῖχεν αὐτῶ τῆς θοίνης. Ἀλα-
ρ δαιΐοῶντος δὲ Ίοὺ θηρλτικοῦ κακεῖ-
νον ὀνϕδίζοντος. ὅτε αὐτὸς μὰν κα-
θ᾽ἐκάς΄ην μοχθᾷ, ἐκεῖνος δέ μκδὲν
πονῶν Ίοῖς αὐΐοῦ τρέφειΐ πόνοις, ῦ-
πολαβὼν αὐ Ίὸς ἔπε. μὴ ἐ μὲ᾽, ἀλλὰ
Ίον δεαπότην μέμϕϫ. ὃς οὐ πονῦ ῆμⲋ

THE TWO DOGS

(Folios 49r–49v)

There once was a man who had two
dogs. One he trained as a hunter, and the
other he trained as a guard dog. Whenever the hunter brought back some game
from the chase, his master always made
a point of throwing some of it to the
guard dog. The hunter became increas-
ingly annoyed with this state of affairs,
and made his feelings known to the
guard dog. He pointed out that it was
his duty to go out in both fair weather
and foul to hunt, while the guard dog
didn't do anything except lie around–
and still he was rewarded with game.
When the guard dog had heard enough,
he responded: "Don't blame me, I'm
not the one who has decided to do things
this way. It was our master who decided
that you should hunt and that I should
share in your prey."

The moral of this fable is: So, too, one
should not blame children who are lazy,
when it is their parents who have made
them so.

f. 49r

THE MAN AND THE SHREW

(Folios 49v–50r)

A man was married to a woman who
made life miserable for the entire household. He wondered whether she would
behave the same way in his father's
house, so he made up an excuse and sent
her to stay with his father. After a few
days she returned home and he asked her
how she had been treated by his father's
servants. "For some reason," she responded, "the herdsmen and the shep-
herds seemed to be annoyed with me."
Her husband then said: "If people
you saw only at the beginning and the
end of the day had trouble with you,
what do you think it must be like
for those who must spend all day long
in your company?"

The moral of this fable is: Minor actions
may often teach major lessons and
obvious motives may reveal hidden ones.

ῷς πρὸς Τοῖς ἐκῇ διαλέγω· τῆς δὲ
φαμένης ὡς οἱ βουκόλοι καὶ οἱ ποι-
μένες ἀπεβλέποντο, πρὸς αὐτὴν ἔφη. ἀλλ' ὡς ἴωμεν, ὁ τοῖς ζο δ'
σωζόμεναι, οἱ ὄρθρου μὲν Τὰς ποίμν
ἐξελαύνοσιν, ὁ δὲ δὲ εἰσιασιν, τί
χρὴ προσδοκᾶν ποει Τουτων, οἷς
πᾶσαν σὺ ὡς δι' εἰ βοῦ Τὴν ἡμέρ δι·
ἐπιμύθιον·
ὁ μῦθος δηλοῖ, ὅ τὸ οὕτω πολλάκις
ἐκ Τῶν μικρῶν Τὰ μεγάλα, καὶ ἐκ
Των προδήλων Τὰ ἄδηλα γνωείζ.

ῥίφος καὶ λύκος·
ῥίφος ὑστερήσας Τῆς ποίμνης,
ὑπὸ λύκου καταδιώκετο· ἐπι-

THE KID AND THE FLUTE-PLAYING WOLF
(Folios 50r–50v)

A kid wandered away from his mother and into the forest, where he soon found himself being stalked by a wolf. He began to run, calling over his shoulder to the wolf: "I know that I am destined to be your dinner, but before I die I would like you to do me a favor. Please play the flute, so that I may meet my end dancing." The wolf decided to oblige the kid and began to play a flute, which he just happened to have with him. The sound of his playing attracted the attention of a pack of dogs, however, and when they saw the wolf they began to give chase. As he fled, the wolf called back to the kid: "Well, it's all my own fault, for I am a butcher by trade, and had no business playing a flutist."

The moral of this fable is: Those whose behavior is not adapted to the particular circumstances in which they find themselves, may discover they have lost something that seemed to be already within their grasp.

THE CRAB AND THE FOX

(*Folios 50v–51r*)

A crab crawled up onto the shore in
search of a private and peaceful place
in which to live, far from the hurly-
burly of the sea. Unfortunately, a famished fox noticed him, gave chase, and
soon caught the crab. On the verge of
death, the crab cried out: "I am getting
just what I deserve. I am a sea creature,
I had no business trying to change myself into a land dweller."

The moral of this fable is: So, too, with
human beings–those who abandon
the work for which they are suited, and
go off to try to do things for which they
are unequipped, soon find themselves
completely lost.

51

THE ZITHER PLAYER
(Folios 51r–51v)

There once was a zither player who was hopelessly lacking in talent—but that didn't stop him from practicing all day long at home. His house had thick walls and the echo they created gave him the impression that he played well. So taken was he with this fantasy that he decided to rent a theater and give a public performance. When he actually appeared, however, he played so badly that the audience drove him from the stage with a barrage of stones.

The moral of this fable is: So, too, with certain individuals who seem to have a certain facility in public speaking when they are in school, but when they venture to address a general audience, they fall flat on their faces.

THE THIEVES AND THE ROOSTER

(Folios 51v–52r)

When a gang of robbers broke into a house one day, the only thing they could find to steal was a rooster, so they carried him off. As they were about to kill and eat him, he cried out, begging that his life be spared. He claimed that he was actually quite useful, since his crowing awakened people so that they could rise early for work. The thieves responded that this was an excellent reason for them to slaughter him, since, by waking people up, he could prevent them from being robbed.

The moral of this fable is: One man's Mede is another man's Persian.

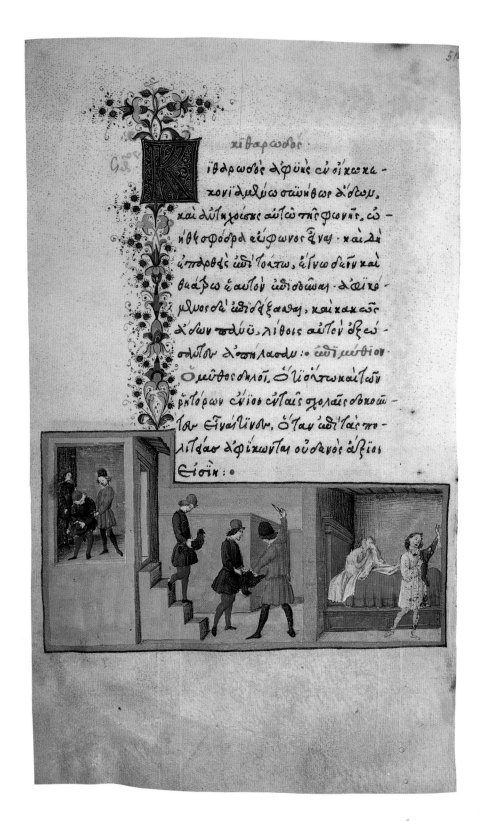

52

THE CROW AND THE RAVEN
(*Folios 52r–52v*)

A crow grew jealous of a raven who was held in high esteem by men because he foretold the future. The crow desired the same respect, and so, when he saw some passersby, he perched in a tree near them and gave voice to a series of raucous cries. At first, when they heard all the commotion, the people were frightened, until one man realized that the sounds were coming from a crow and said to the others: "Pay no attention. Those screeches have no significance."

The moral of this fable is: So, too, is it among men—those who attempt to rival their betters wind up not only failing, but also subjecting themselves to ridicule.

f. 52r

121

THE ROOK AND THE DOG

(Folios 52v–53r)

A rook offered a sacrifice to Athena and invited a dog to the feast that customarily followed the event. The dog asked the bird: "Why do you waste your possessions on useless sacrifices? That goddess detests you enough to prove all your omens false." The rook replied: "But that is precisely why I offer sacrifices to her—I know she doesn't like me and I am trying to win her over."

The moral of this fable is: So, too, many people will offer gifts to enemies whom they fear.

κορώνη καὶ κόων·

ορώνη ἀθηνᾶ θύος ᾶ, κ ω ἀ ωδ
ὅτι ἀοιδ ἐκάλ· ὁ δέ, πρὸς αὐτ
ἔφ , τί μά οι τὰς θυσίας ἀναλίσκεις.
ἡ γὰρ θεὸς οὕτω ἀ εῖοῦ, ὡς κ κ τ ῶν
ἐ ρόφωνα οἰωνῶν τὴν πίστι μ ἀ-
χ εῖν· καὶ ἡ κορώνη πρὸς αὐτόν. διὰ
το π μ ηγ αὐτῇ θύω ἵνα ιλα ωτ ῆ

Ε πιμ θιον·

ὁ μῦθος δηλοῖ, ὅτι πολλοὶ διὰ κέρδ
τοῖς ἐχθροῖς ωφ ῶν· οὐκ ὀκνο οῦσιν·

κόραξ καὶ ὄφις·

ὁ ραξ ροφ ς ἀπορῶν, ὡς κ τ -
δεν ἐν τινι λ ίω τόπω ὄφιν
κοιμώμενον, το π καταπ τὰς ἡρ-

THE CROW AND THE SNAKE
(Folios 53r–53v)

A crow, desperate for something to eat,
spied a snake dozing in the sun. He
pounced on the reptile and then flew off
with it. The serpent awakened with a
start, and bit the bird. As the crow ex-
pired, he cried out: "I thought I had
found salvation, instead I have found
death."

The moral of this fable is: So, too, with
men who look for treasure and lose
their lives.

f. 53r

THE JACKDAW AND THE PIGEONS

(Folios 53v–54r)

A jackdaw had noticed that the pigeons who lived in a nearby coop were very well fed. So, he whitened his feathers and joined them, hoping to share in their rich meals. In order not to betray himself, he was very quiet, and—at first— the pigeons were fooled by his disguise. In fact, they even held him in some esteem. But, one day, the jackdaw forgot where he was and gave his familiar cry, at which the pigeons chased him away. Dejected, he returned to his fellow jackdaws, but they mistook him for a pigeon and also chased him away. Thus, by trying to share in the food of two different kinds of birds, the jackdaw wound up with none.

The moral of this fable is: We ought to be content with what we are, avoiding that envy which will not only fail to make us something else, but may actually bring ruin upon us.

f. 53v

54

THE JACKDAW AT LARGE
(Folios 54r–54v)

A man captured a jackdaw, tied a string to one of its legs, and gave the bird to his child as a pet. The jackdaw had no interest in living the life of a plaything, however, and made his escape at the first opportunity, returning to his nest. Unfortunately, the string remained attached to his leg and, one day, it became caught in the branch of a tree, holding the bird fast so that he could not fly away. The jackdaw saw that all was lost and moaned: "I gave up the life of a slave among men to die like this in the wild."

The moral of this fable is: Beware of trying to save yourself from some minor danger, and thereby losing your life.

HERMES AND THE CRAFTSMEN
(Folios 54v–55r)

Zeus gave Hermes the task of poisoning the character of all craftsmen with the tendency to lie. Hermes compounded his poison and measured out an equal portion for each craft. But he made too much and, after he had given every craftsman except the shoemaker his dose, he found that he had a great deal left over. So he gave everything that remained to the shoemaker. As a result, all craftsmen are liars, but shoemakers are the biggest liars of all.

The moral of this fable is: Any liar might try this tale on for size.

f. 54v

f. 55r

ZEUS AND MODESTY
(*Folios 55r–55v*)

When Zeus made man he endowed him with many virtues, but one–Modesty–he forgot. He thought about how he might rectify this error, and decided that she should enter man through his behind. Naturally, Modesty was indignant, not to mention revolted, by such a suggestion. But Zeus insisted, and so she said: "All right, I'll take that route in, but only on the condition that Eros can't do it too. If he comes along, I'm leaving."

The moral of this fable is: There's a good reason why certain people are shameless.

ZEUS AND THE TORTOISE

(*Folios 55v–56r*)

Zeus gave a party to celebrate his marriage, and he invited all the animals to attend. Everyone came—except the tortoise. The next day, Zeus summoned the tortoise and demanded to know why he had stayed away. The tortoise responded: "There's no place like home." Hearing this, the god became angry, and condemned the tortoise to carry his house with him wherever he went.

The moral of this fable is: However humble or haughty, there are many who share the tortoise's opinion!

λυκος και πεοβαλον·

f. 56r

THE WOUNDED WOLF AND THE EWE
(Folios 56r–56v)

Having been attacked and wounded by a pack of dogs, a wolf was lying exhausted on the ground. Since he was unable to find food in his usual manner, he was forced to try other methods. He saw a ewe and asked her to bring him some water from a nearby stream. "If you bring me something to drink, I'll find something to eat on my own," he said. But the ewe replied: "If I give you something to drink, I'll be your main course."

The moral of this fable is: Beware of the evil that lurks beneath the words of hypocrites.

THE HARES AND THE FOXES
(*Folios 56v–57r*)

The hares were having a battle with the eagles, and they asked the foxes to help them. The foxes answered: "We would come to your aid if we didn't know just who you are, and exactly who it is you are fighting."

The moral of this fable is: Anyone who engages in warfare against those who are obviously stronger will encounter difficulties in the search for allies.

f. 56v

THE ANT
(Folios 57r–57v)

The creature we call the ant was, once upon a time, a farmer who was not content with the fruits of his own labors—so he stole those of his neighbors. Noting this behavior, Zeus became angry, and transformed the man into an ant. Despite the fact that the creature's outward appearance had changed, however, his character had not. To this day, he still scurries through the fields and steals the wheat and barley, just as he did when he was a man.

The moral of this fable is: However clever the disguise, character will out.

THE BAT AND THE WEASELS
(*Folios 57v–58r*)

When a bat slipped off its perch and fell to the ground, a watchful weasel snapped him up immediately. Seeing that the end was near, the bat begged for mercy. The weasel replied that this was impossible, since he and the bat were natural enemies. In fact, the weasel added, the bat was his worst enemy among all the birds. The bat protested that he wasn't actually a bird at all, but a sort of flying mouse, and so the weasel let him go. Another time, the same bat fell again and was grabbed by a different weasel, who made it clear that he intended to eat the bat, since he hated mice. The bat told this weasel that, while he might look like a mouse, he really was not a rodent. So, once again, he was set free. Thus, by changing his name twice, the bat saved his life both times.

The moral of this fable is: Be flexible in the face of danger.

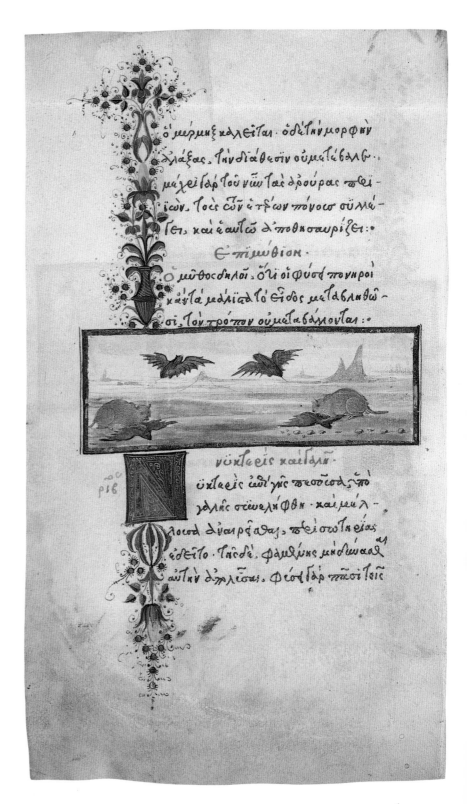

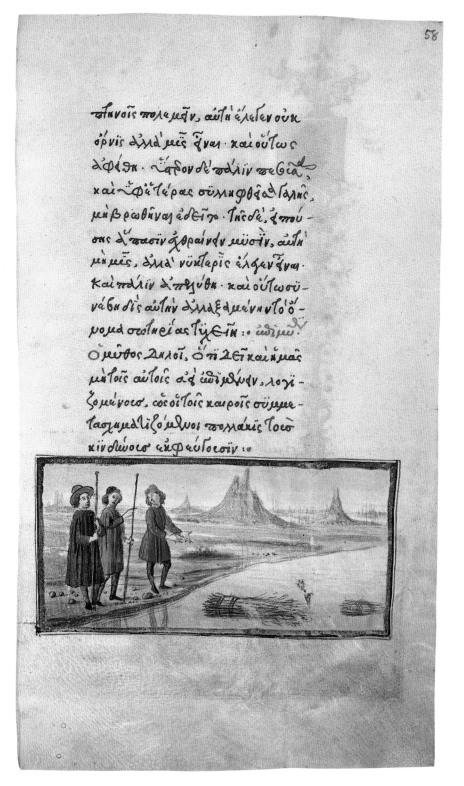

58

THE TRAVELERS AND THE FLOTSAM
(Folios 58r–58v)

One day, some travelers were making their way along the seashore. Looking out over the water, they saw some flotsam, which they mistook for a great warship. As the flotsam flowed nearer, they changed their minds and thought that it wasn't a warship, but a freighter. When the flotsam floated ashore, however, they were finally able to see exactly what it was. Looking at one another, the travelers exclaimed: "What fools we were to spend all this time looking at nothing!"

The moral of this fable is: Some men seem impressive at first, but close inspection soon reveals how ordinary they really are.

THE WILD DONKEY AND THE TAME ONE
(Folios 58v–59r)

A wild donkey envied the lot of a tame donkey who enjoyed pleasant circumstances and good food. But soon, the wild donkey began to notice how hard the other donkey had to work. He saw the poor beast carrying heavy burdens, and being whipped frequently by his owner with a big stick. Then the wild donkey realized that his envy was baseless, considering the price the tame donkey had to pay for his "advantages."

The moral of this fable is: There is nothing enviable in a lifestyle that provides certain comforts, but only in return for much pain and suffering.

f. 58v

ὄνος ἄρειος ·

νος ἄρειος ἄνον ἰδὼν ἡμίονον ἐ-
τῖνι ἀλλήλω τόπω. πρεσβε
αὐτὸν ἐμακάριζεν, ἰωτ τε τῆ διαει
τοῦ σώματος καὶ τῆ τῆς ῦρφῆς ἀπο-
λαύσει. ὕστερον δὲ ἰδὼν αὐτὸν ἀ-
χθοφοροῦντα, καὶ τὸν ὀνηλάτην
ὄπισθεν ἑπόμενον, καὶ ῥοπάλοις
αὐτὸν παίοντα ἔφη. ἀλλ' ἔγωγε
οὐκέτι σε εὐδαιμονίζω. ὁρῶ γὰρ
ὡς οὐκ ἄνευ κακῶν μεγάλων τὴν εὐ-
δαιμονίαν ἔχεις. ὁ λῦτος δηλοῖ.
ὁ μῦτος δηλοῖ, ὅτι οὐκ ἔστι ζῆλω-
τὰ τὰ μετὰ κινδύνων καὶ ταλαιπω-
ρειῶν κέρδη. ◦

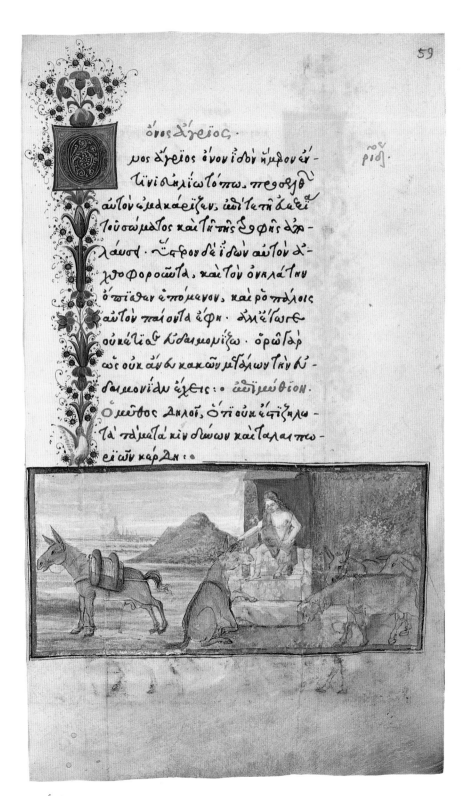

f. 59r

THE DONKEYS' PETITION TO
ZEUS
(Folios 59r–59v)

The donkeys had become weary of always
having to carry heavy burdens and,
consequently, of always being exhausted.
So, one day, they sent envoys to Zeus
to ask him to alleviate their suffering.
Zeus knew that this would be impossible,
but—to soothe them—he proposed an
improbable solution to their woe. He
told them that their misery would end
when a river was formed out of their
urine. The donkeys took this prophecy
seriously and, to this day, when one of
them sees the stream of another donkey's
urine, he stops—and adds a little something to it.

The moral of this fable is: One's destiny
cannot be avoided.

THE FOX, AND THE DONKEY
DISGUISED AS A LION
(Folios 59v–6or)

A donkey disguised himself by putting
on a lion's skin. He then went around
frightening his fellow animals. When he
saw a fox, the donkey decided to scare
him as well. But the fox, who knew the
difference between a donkey's bray and
a lion's roar, said: "There's no doubt
about it. I, too, would be afraid of you—
if I hadn't heard your voice."

The moral of this fable is: So, too, with
the uneducated, who try to pretend to
greater knowledge than they possess—
their words soon give them away.

f. 59v

ὄνος καὶ βάτραχοι.

f. 60r

THE DONKEY AND THE FROGS
(Folios 60r–60v)

A donkey loaded down beneath a heavy stack of wood was making his way through a swamp. At one point, he slipped and fell and couldn't get back up. He began to moan and groan. The frogs who lived in the swamp heard his cries and said: "You seem terribly sorry for yourself. You slip and fall into this swamp once and you whimper like an infant. What sort of noises would you make if you had to live here all the time, as we do?"

The moral of this fable is: Complainers, take note of this tale.

THE DONKEY, THE CROW, AND THE WOLF

(*Folios 60v–61r*)

A donkey with a cut on his back was wandering through a field. Along came a crow who settled on the animal's back, and began pecking at the wound. The donkey began to bray loudly and kick wildly as the pain increased. His master– on the other side of the field–saw what was happening and started to laugh. A wolf, who spied the enraged donkey, muttered to himself: "All people have to do is catch sight of us in passing, and they begin to hunt us down. But the antics of this donkey, behaving like a maniac, just make them laugh."

The moral of this fable is: A true evil-doer is usually recognizable.

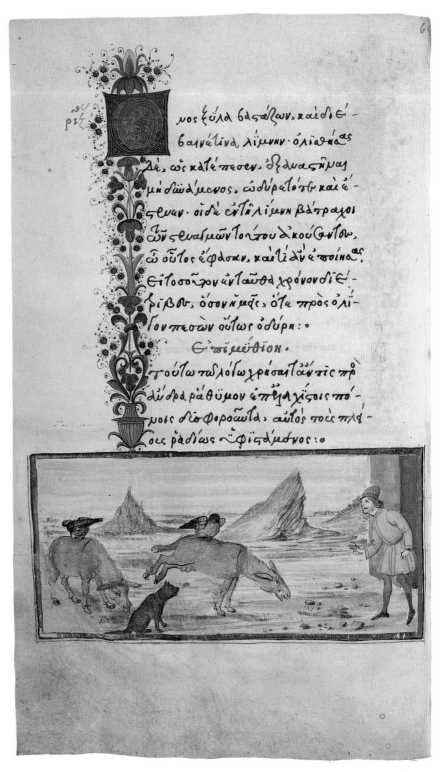

ὄνος καὶ κόραξ

νος ἠλκωμένος τὸν νῶτον, εὐ-
τινι χειμῶνι ἀνέμῳ. κόρα ος
δὲ ἐπ᾽ αὐτὸν διόδευλος αὐτῷ, καὶ τὸ
ἕλκος ξαίνοντος, ὁ ὄνος ὠρᾶτο καὶ
ἤλατο. τοῦ δὲ ὀνηλάτου πόρρωθεν
ἱστᾳμένου καὶ τὸ γελῶντος, λύκος πα-
ρειὼν αὐτὸν εἶδε καὶ ἔφη. ἄθλιοι
ἡμεῖς, κἂν μόνον ὀφθῶμεν αὐτῷ
διωκώμεθα. τοῦ τῳ δὲ καὶ πε ρ
σαινομένου καταγελῶσιν :· ἐπιμύθιον .
ὁ μῦθος δηλοῖ, ὅτι οἱ κακοῦργοι
τῶν ἀνθρώπων καὶ μόνον φαινόμε ε
δῆλοι εἰσίν :·

ὄνος καὶ ἀλώπηξ .

61

THE DONKEY, THE FOX, AND THE LION
(Folios 61r–61v)

A donkey and a fox became friends and set out together to hunt. On the way, they met a lion. Sensing danger, the fox went up to the lion and whispered to the king of beasts that he could have the donkey, if only the lion wouldn't eat him at the same time. The lion said that seemed reasonable. So the fox led the donkey into a trap, causing him to fall into a ditch from which he couldn't escape. The lion, seeing that he was certain to have the donkey in any case, picked up the fox and threw him into the ditch too.

The moral of this fable is: Beware of setting traps for your friends, for you may find yourself caught in them as well.

f. 61r

THE HEN AND THE SWALLOW

(Folios 61v–62r)

A hen happened upon a snake's eggs and began to treat them as her own. Carefully, she settled down over them and, thus warmed, they soon hatched. A swallow noted what the hen had done and said to her: "What a fool you are. Why did you give life to creatures who—once they are grown—will pierce you with their serpents' teeth?"

The moral of this fable is: One should not expect good deeds to have much effect on bad eggs.

f. 61v

62

THE FIRST APPEARANCE OF THE CAMEL
(*Folios 62r–62v*)

When they encountered a camel for the first time, men were very much afraid. In fact, they were so intimidated by its great size that they actually fled in terror. After a while, however, they became aware of the camel's potential usefulness, and they tamed both their fear and the animal. Once it became a beast of burden, their fear changed to contempt, and they even let little children lead the camel around with a bridle.

The moral of this fable is: As we become more familiar with things, our fears diminish.

THE STEPPED-ON SERPENT
(Folios 62v–63r)

There was a serpent who was constantly being stepped on by people. He grew very tired of this and went to Zeus with his complaint. Zeus told him: "If you had bitten the first person who stepped on you, everyone else would have trod more carefully."

The moral of this fable is: Fight your battles early on and you will have fewer to fight in the days that follow.

f. 62v

142

ὁ δὲ ἔλᾶς πρὸς αὐτὸν ἔιπεν. ἀπέι
τον πεθῆρον παῖνοδύῃ ἔ ωληξ,
οὐ κᾶν ὁ σῆπδος ἔ τεχάρηα τοῦτο
ποιῆσαι :· ἰωῆμεῦθιον.
ὁ μεῦθος λκλοῖ, ὁ ὒ οι τοῖς πε-
τρον ἰωῆ βαίνοσιν λυθίς ἀ μελνοι,
τοῖς ἄλλοις φοβαροὶ ΐίνονται :·

σεῖσερά·

σεῖσερά οἵ τα σιω ᾠρμλιν, ὡς
ἐθεάζατο ἀν τινι τὸ πεσ κρᾶ -
τῆρα ὕ οἴλιος τερφμμλνον, ἐχόμι-
σιν ἀληθιῶν ἔιναι. δῖ ὁ καὶ πολ-
λῶ τῶ ρῴζω ἐνεχθεᾶ, ἐλθαν
ζ αὐτὸν τῷ πίνμνι αμπεσῖᾶ,
ὡς καὶ τῶ σταρῶν αὐτᾶς πεῖπλ -

THE THIRSTY DOVE
(*Folios 63r–63v*)

A dove, overcome by thirst, mistook a
wall painting depicting a pool of water
for the real thing. In her haste to get a
drink she flew into the painting—and
crashed to the ground with a thud. The
painter, who was nearby, picked her up
and ate her for dinner.

The moral of this fable is: So, too,
certain people rush madly into things
without thinking, and wind up having
their wings clipped.

f. 63r

THE DOVE AND THE CROW

(*Folios 63v–64r*)

A dove who had been raised in a dove-cote was boasting about the number of chicks she had borne. A crow overheard her bragging and remarked: "I wouldn't be so pleased with myself if I were you, for—if you think about it—the more children you have, the more doves you condemn to captivity."

The moral of this fable is: Thus it is also with servants—the unhappiest are those who have the most children in service.

f. 63v

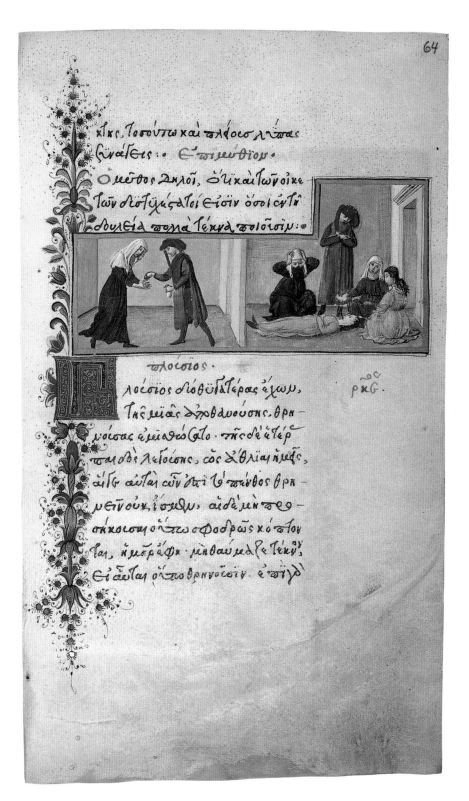

64

THE RICH MAN AND THE MOURNERS
(Folios 64r–64v)

A rich man had two daughters. When one of them died, he hired professional mourners to keen at her burial. This prompted his other daughter to remark to her mother: "What a sorrowful situation! We grieve but we don't cry, while these mourners–who didn't even know my sister–are weeping loudly and beating their breasts." Her mother answered: "Don't let it upset you, my dear, these mourners may seem to be crying their hearts out, but to them, it's only work-for-hire."

The moral of this fable is: So, too, will certain people (whenever they have the opportunity), try to profit from the misfortunes of others.

f. 64r

THE SHEPHERD AND HIS SHEEP

(Folios 64v–65r)

A shepherd herded his flock into the forest to let them feed on acorns. Deep in the woods, he came upon a great oak tree that was laden with nuts. He stretched his cloak out under the tree and then climbed up and knocked the acorns to the ground. The sheep immediately began to gobble up these treats and, in their enthusiasm, they ate the shepherd's cloak as well. When the shepherd saw what they had done, he berated his flock, crying: "You wicked animals! You give the wool off your backs to strangers for their clothing. But I, who feed you and look after you, I don't even have a cloak anymore, thanks to you!"

The moral of this fable is: So, too, many people make every effort to oblige those who have done nothing for them, while they behave very badly toward others who have treated them with kindness.

f. 64v

65

THE FISHERMAN AND THE MINNOW
(Folios 65r–65v)

A fisherman cast his net in the ocean and caught a minnow. The minnow begged the fisherman to throw him back, claiming that he was really too small to be of any use to anyone. The minnow then suggested to the fisherman that he should return later when he would find a fully-grown fish that he could catch and sell at a good profit. But the fisherman was having none of this. "Far better," he said, "to have a minnow in the net than the remote possibility of a whale in the future."

The moral of this fable is: Take advantage of what is at hand even if it seems meager, and don't disregard it in the hope that something better may come along sometime in the future.

THE HORSE AND THE DONKEY
(*Folios 65v–66r*)

There was a man who owned a horse and a donkey. One day, he loaded them up with goods–especially the donkey–and set out with the two animals. As they trudged along, the donkey said to the horse: "If you value my life, please take some of this burden from me." But the horse ignored the other animal's request. A little while later, the donkey fell dead in his tracks. The man then added the donkey's burden to the load the horse was already carrying and, having skinned the dead animal, threw the donkey's skin over the top of the pile. The horse groaned: "What a foolish beast I am. I refused to help the donkey and now I am carrying his burden, as well as my own–with his skin thrown in as a booby prize."

The moral of this fable is: By making common cause, both the strong and the weak can render their burdens more bearable.

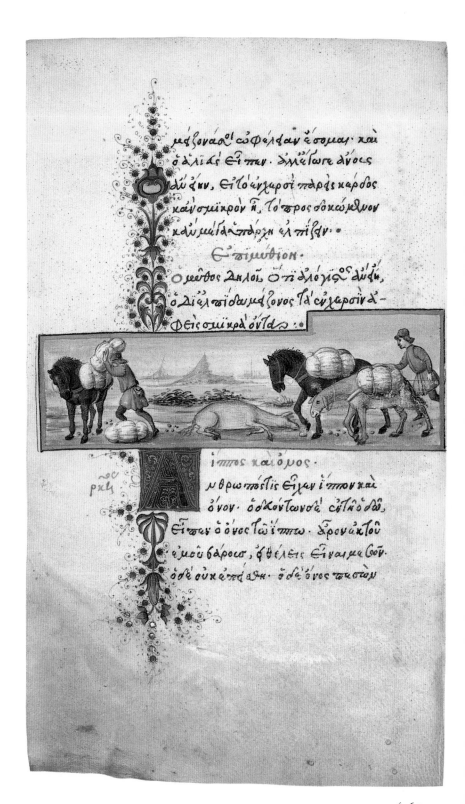

f. 65v

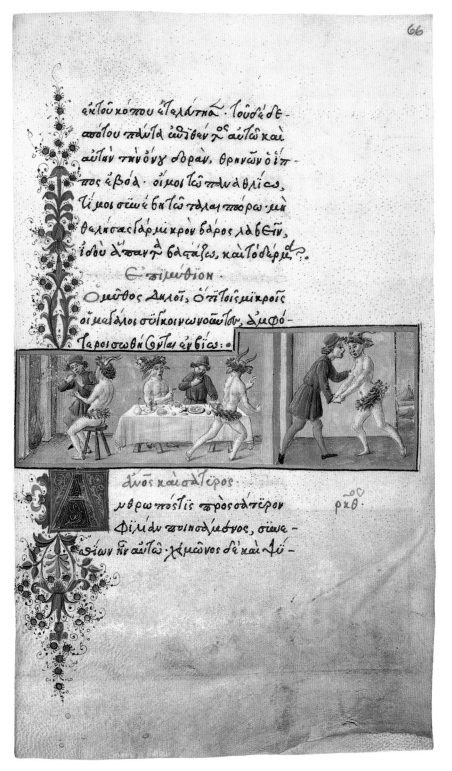

f. 66r

THE MAN AND THE SATYR
(Folios 66r–66v)

It is said that there was once a man who had formed a close friendship with a satyr. But on a certain winter day, when they were out together strolling in the woods, the man–feeling cold–put his hands to his mouth and blew on them. The satyr asked why he was doing this. The man answered that he was trying to warm his hands. Later that same day, at dinner, they were served some stew straight from a boiling pot. The man took a spoonful and blew on it before he began to eat. The satyr again asked the man what he was doing. The man explained that he was cooling his food. "Well, that finishes our friendship," declared the satyr, "since you blow hot and cold with the same breath."

The moral of this fable is: Remember the satyr's words when listening to your friends–or those whom you suppose to be your friends.

THE FOX AND THE WOOD CUTTER

(*Folios 66v–67v*)

A fox, in flight from a pack of hunters, came upon a woodcutter and begged him for help. The woodcutter told the fox that he could hide in a nearby shed. A few moments later, the hunters came along and asked the woodcutter if he had seen a fox. The man told them that he hadn't seen any fox, but—as he spoke— he gestured toward the shed. The hunters failed to notice his gesture and went

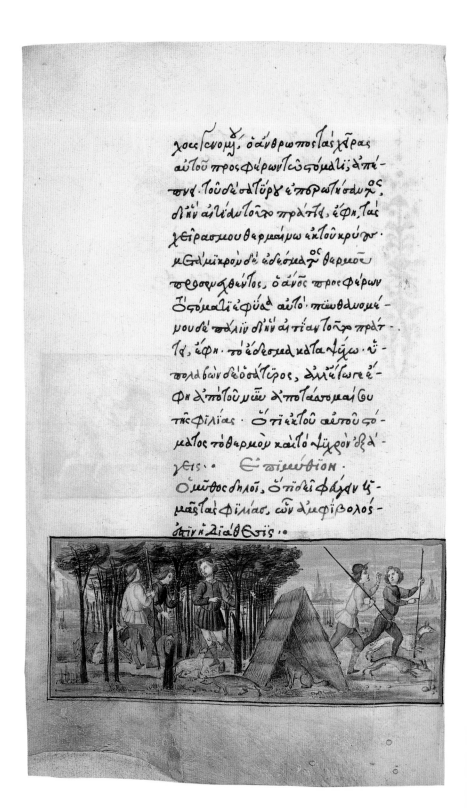

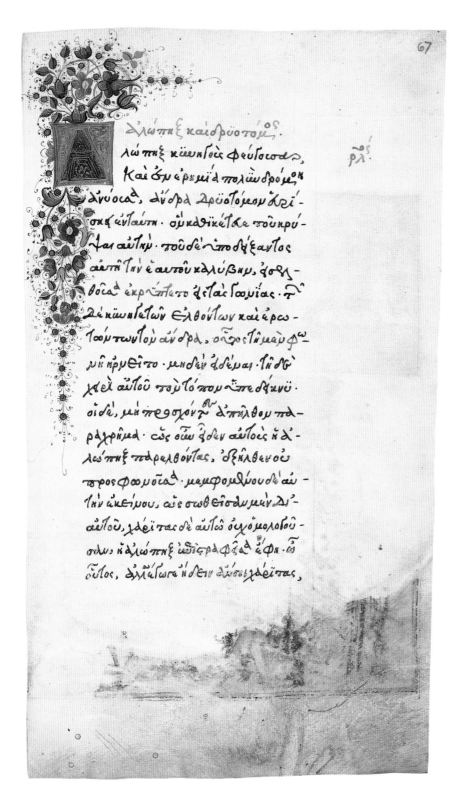

away. But the fox noticed it. As the animal emerged from the shed and began to move away, the woodcutter asked him why he had no word of thanks for the help he had received. The fox responded: "I would have thanked you, if your actions had matched your words."

The moral of this fable is: Had the fox chosen to respond more succinctly, he might have used just one word–"Hypocrite."

THE MAN WHO BROKE THE STATUE

(Folios 67v–68r)

Once, there was a man who owned a wooden statue of a god. Since he was poor, he was constantly praying to the god to bestow riches upon him. But his prospects did not improve and, after a while, he became so angry that—in a fit of rage—he picked up the statue and smashed it against the wall. As it broke open, the statue revealed that it was filled with gold. Happily, the man picked up the gold and said: "Well, dear god, you seem to have everything backward. When I prayed to you, you did nothing for me. When I reviled you, you rewarded me."

The moral of this fable is: One does better to take a whack at a dishonest man than to ask him for favors.

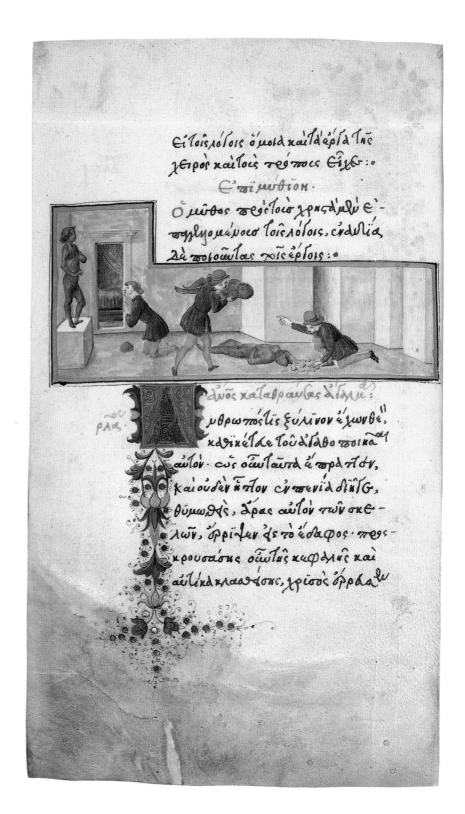

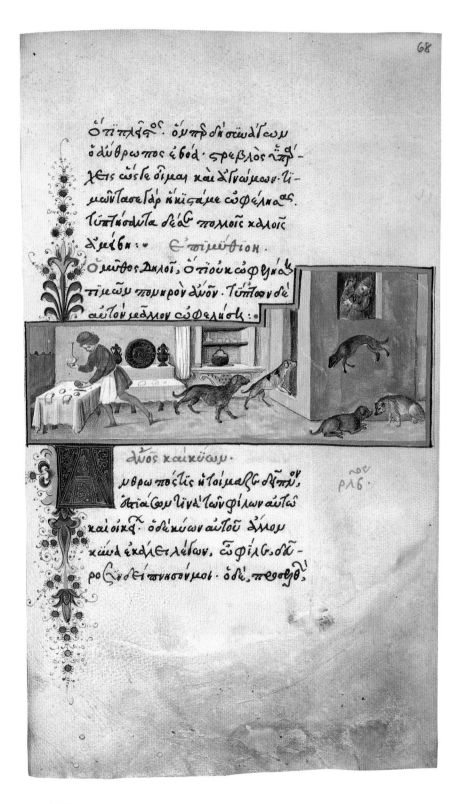

f. 68r

THE DOG WHO CAME TO DINNER
(Folios 68r–69r)

A man was preparing a dinner for some friends, and his dog invited a friend as well. The latter arrived full of anticipation and, when he saw the splendid array of food, he said to himself: "What an unexpected pleasure! I am going to stuff myself so that I won't be able to eat again for days." While he stood there talking to himself, wagging his tail (the very image of man's best friend), the cook noticed how much attention the dog was paying to the food. Without hesitation, he grabbed the animal by the paws and threw him out the window. As the dog went yelping home, he met another dog along the way, who asked him how the dinner had been. The disinvited guest responded: "It couldn't have been better. I became so rip-roaring drunk that I'm not even sure how I got here!"

The moral of this fable is: Even dogs have to save face sometimes.

χαῖρ' ἵνα τὸ βλέπων τὸν μέγαν δαίμονον,
βοῶν ἐν τῇ καρδία. βαβαὶ πόσημοι
χρῆν ἀρτίως ὅταν τῖναίως ἐφάνη· ρα-
φίσομαι ἐς γὰρ καὶ ἐς κόρον δει-
τωνίσω, ὡς ἐτέμες αὐτὸν μηδαμῆ
γε τῇ νάσαι. ταῦτα κατ' ἐμαυτὸν λέ-
γοντος τοῦ κύωνος, καὶ ἅμα ὁ φ'οντος
τὴν κέρκον. ὡς ἂν εἰς τὸν φίλον
θαρσῶντος, ὁ μάγειρος ὡς εἶδε τὸ
τοῖον ὧδε κἀκεῖσε τὴν κέρκον
σείς γράφοντα, καὶ ἐς χεῖρα ὅς ἑ-
λὼν αὐτοῦ, ὁ ῥίψας παραχρῆμα
ἐξω τῶν θυρίδων. ὁ δὲ καὶ ἰὼν δ-
τοῦ μεγάλως πραξων. τῶν τις δὲ
κύωνῶν, ἐν κἀς τὸ δοὺ αὐτὸς συνδ-
ιόντων, ἐρωτᾷ δὲ πῶς ἐδείπνη-
σας φίλος. ὁ δὲ πρὸς αὐτὸν ὑπο-
λαβὼν ἔφη. ὑπὸ τὸς πολλῆς πόσως
μεθυσθεὶς ὑπὲρ κόρον οὐδὲ ᾗ
ὁδοῦ αὐτὴν ὅθεν ἐξῆλθον οἶδα:·

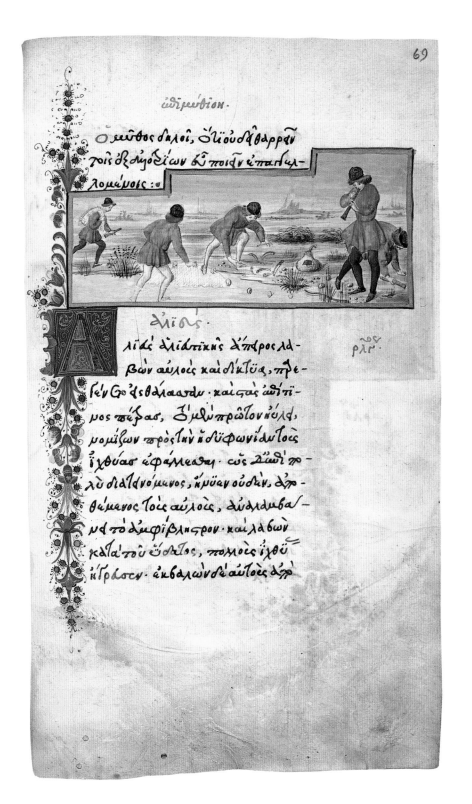

f. 69r

THE FISHERMAN WHO PLAYED THE FLUTE

(Folios 69r–69v)

There once was a fisherman who enjoyed playing the flute. One day, he went down to the sea carrying both his nets and his musical instrument. When he reached the shoreline, he sat down on a rock that jutted out over the sea and began to play the flute. He thought that the sweetness of his music would so beguile the fish that they would leap up onto the shore and become stranded. Things did not work out as he had hoped, however. After a long solo performance, he had not landed a single minnow. So he put his flute aside, picked up his nets, and began to fish in the conventional manner. He soon brought in a big haul and—as he dragged the overflowing nets onto the sand—some of the fish leapt out onto the shore. Seeing them flail about on the ground, the fisherman remarked: "Oh, what contrary creatures you are. When I played the flute for you, you wouldn't dance. Now that I've stopped playing, you're hopping about."

The moral of this fable is: When faced with adversity, there are those who can only wave their arms and shout—but to no avail.

THE COWHERD AND THE LION
(Folios 69v–70r)

There was a cowherd who lost a calf
from among the herd of cattle he was
tending. Having conducted a fruitless
search for the animal, he prayed to Zeus
for help–promising to sacrifice a goat
to the god if he recovered the calf. Later,
as he was walking through the woods,
he saw a lion munching on his missing
animal. The cowherd, beside himself
with fear, raised his arms to the sky and
pleaded: "Oh, god in heaven, I promised
you a goat if I found my calf. Now I
promise you a bull, if only I can escape
from my discovery."

The moral of this fable is: There are
those who react to embarrassing situations by looking frantically for any way
out, and then flee without thinking about
where their escape route might actually
lead them.

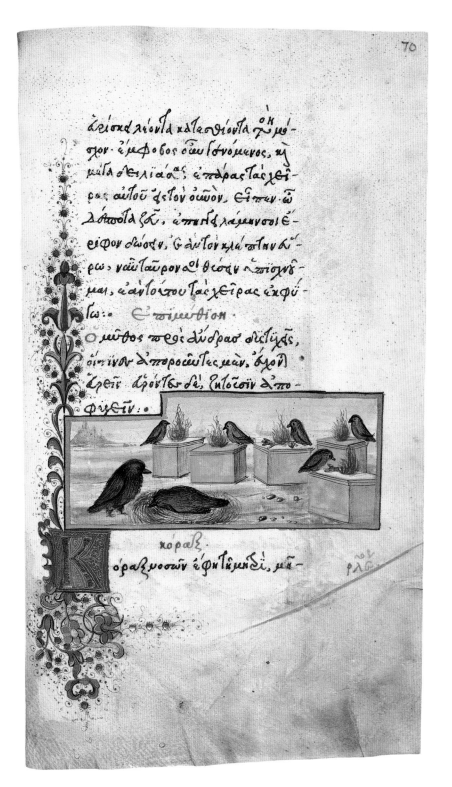

70

THE SICK CROW
(Folios 70r–70v)

A sick crow said to his mother: "Save your tears, mother. Instead, pray to the gods to help me." Tearfully, his mother asked: "Which god, my beloved? Is there a single one of them who will have pity on you? Is there even one from among whose sacrifices you have not stolen some morsel?"

The moral of this fable is: If you should make many enemies in times of good fortune, do not expect to find many friends who will come to your aid in times of misfortune.

f. 70r

THE EAGLE

(*Folios 70v–71r*)

An eagle was perched on an outcropping of rock, scouring the countryside with his eyes, looking for a nice plump hare to eat. A hunter saw him and shot an arrow into his flesh. The arrow penetrated deeply, leaving only the feathers at its end showing on the eagle's breast. Seeing these feathers, the eagle cried out: "That I should die impaled upon another eagle's feathers adds a further sting to the wound."

The moral of this fable is: Sorrow is increased greatly when its source is a familiar one.

f. 71r

THE CRICKET AND THE ANTS
(Folios 71r–71v)

Winter was coming, and the ants were drying their damp grain, preparing it to last them through the cold months. A famished cricket asked the ants if they would give him a little something to eat. The ants replied: "Why didn't you gather food during the summer, as we did, and store it for the barren months ahead?" The cricket replied: "I was too busy making beautiful music." Hearing this, the ants replied: "Well, since you sang during the summer, now you can dance through the winter."

The moral of this fable is: One must be willing to forgo a certain amount of pleasure in the present in order to avoid pain in the future.

THE FOX AND THE WORM
(Folio 71v)

A worm crawled up out of his hole and began to wiggle across the ground. He told the other animals he met along the way that he was a doctor, and possessed the cures for many ills. "In fact," he claimed, "the people of Paeonia consider me a god." A fox who overheard the worm's bragging said: "If you are really so accomplished, why can't you even stand up straight?"

The moral of this fable is: Words count less than deeds.

THE HEN WHO LAID THE GOLDEN EGGS
(Folios 71v–72r)

A man owned a fine hen who laid golden eggs. Thinking that she must have a large supply of gold inside her body, he killed her and cut her open. To his great chagrin, he found nothing except the usual innards. In his eagerness to get rich quickly, he had lost his small but consistent gains.

The moral of this fable is: Patience will bring more rewards than greed.

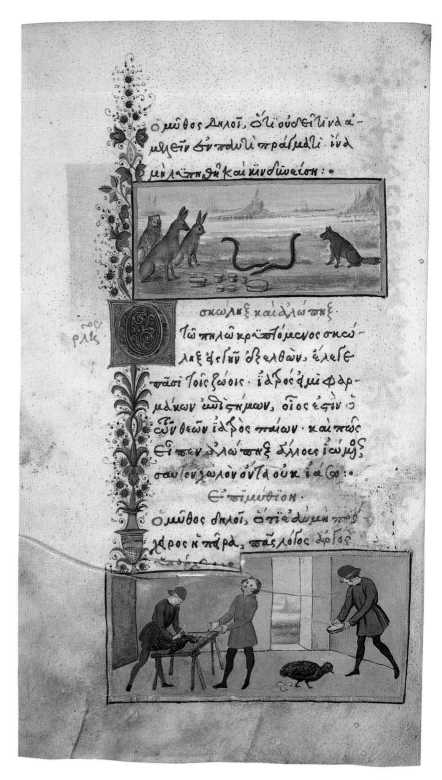

f. 71v

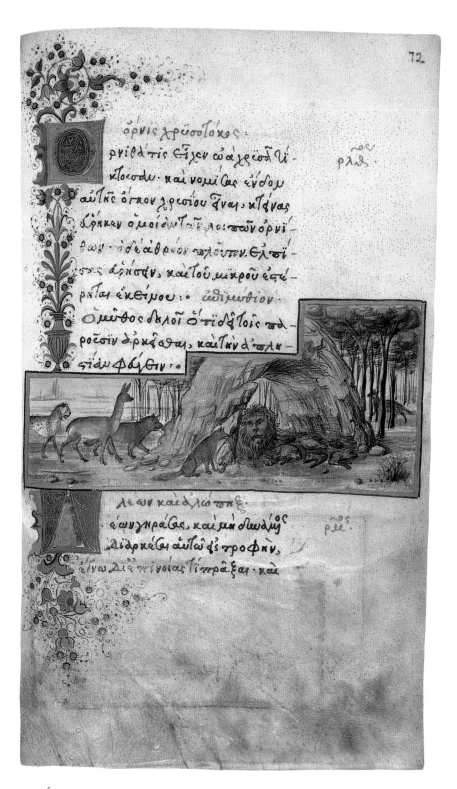

72

THE AGED LION AND THE FOX
(Folios 72r–72v)

Since he had grown old and infirm, a
lion realized that whatever prey he could
no longer hunt with speed and strength
he would have to capture with guile.
So, he took up residence in a cave, pre-
tending to be even more feeble than he
really was. Whenever some unsuspecting
animal wandered by, the lion would
pounce on it and eat it. One day, from
a distance, a fox saw the king of beasts
resting in his cave. He called out to the
lion, asking how he was. "Not very
well," replied the lion, adding an invi-
tation to the fox to approach and spend
some time in the cave with him. "I don't
think so," said the fox, "for it is evident,
by that pile of bones, that many animals
have gone into your cave, but none
seem to have managed to leave."

The moral of this fable is: So, too, do
sensible men heed danger signals, and
watch their steps.

THE WOLF AND THE OLD WOMAN

(Folios 72v–73r)

A hungry wolf was wandering the
countryside in search of something (or
someone) to eat. He came upon an old
woman with a small child and he overheard her say to the little one: "If you
don't stop crying, I am going to feed
you to the wolf." The wolf thought she
was speaking literally, and so he sat down
to wait for his meal. All day he waited,
unobserved by the woman and child.
As dusk fell, the old woman picked up
the child to take him home and, holding
him close, said: "If the big bad wolf
shows up, we will kill him." The literal-
minded wolf heard this and slinked off,
muttering to himself: "Around here,
people say one thing and do another."

The moral of this fable is: Sometimes
it doesn't pay to take people at their word.

f. 72v

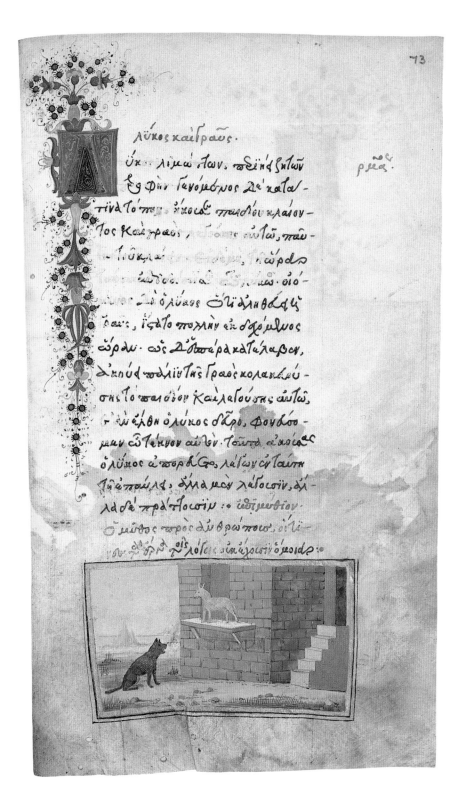

λύκος καὶ ρᾶς.

ρᾶς.

THE GOAT AND THE WOLF
(*Folios 73r–73v*)

A goat was standing on a ledge outside
the window of his owner's house one
day. When he saw a wolf passing by, the
goat began to jeer at the other animal
and call him names. The wolf looked up
and said to the goat: "Miserable creature,
it's not your words that annoy me as
much as the fact that you're beyond
my reach."

The moral of this fable is: There are
times when—with impunity—the weak
may mock the strong.

THE MULE
(Folio 73v)

A mule fattened on barley began to leap about, saying to himself: "My father was a racehorse, so I must be a racehorse too." Then, one day, he found himself forced to run, and—when he finally finished the course—his exhausted panting reminded him of the fact that his father was really a donkey.

The moral of this fable is: Don't forget who and what you are, no matter how strong the temptation to pretend otherwise.

f. 73v

THE TRUMPETER
(*Folio 74r*)

[*Greek text only. The miniature is missing.*]

A trumpeter, whose task it was to sound assembly, was captured by enemy troops. He begged them for mercy, saying: "Please don't kill me. I am no warrior, and I haven't killed any of your soldiers. My trumpet is the only weapon that I possess." But his captors, unmoved by these entreaties, replied: "That is reason enough to kill you, since–although you are not yourself a fighter–you summon others to battle."

The moral of this fable is: Those who urge cruel and wicked leaders to commit evil deeds, deserve death as their punishment.

THE REED AND THE OLIVE TREE
(*Folios 74r–74v*)

The reed and the olive tree were arguing about their respective capacities to withstand adversity, as well as about their individual strength and firmness. At one point, the olive tree sneered at the reed's weakness and its habit of bending before the wind. The reed, however, maintained a polite silence in the face of this rudeness. Just then, a gale-force wind blew up and the reed shook and swayed, but remained firmly rooted. It was the stiff old olive tree that broke in two and smashed to the ground.

The moral of this fable is: Bend to the pressures exerted by those more powerful than you are, or suffer the consequences.

THE WOLF AND THE HERON
(Folios 74v–75r)

Once there was a wolf who had a bone stuck in his throat. He asked a heron to remove it for him, and promised the bird a reward. The heron agreed, and–putting his head down the wolf's throat–pulled out the bone. He then asked the wolf for his reward. The wolf answered: "You still have your head, don't you? Consider that payment enough."

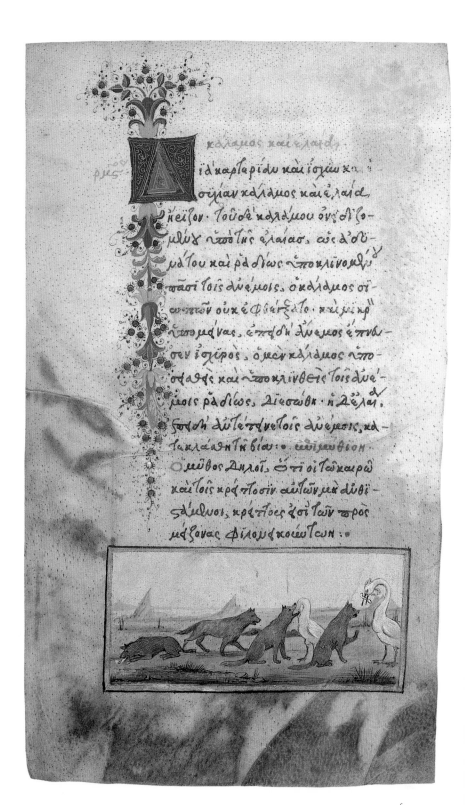

f. 74v

166

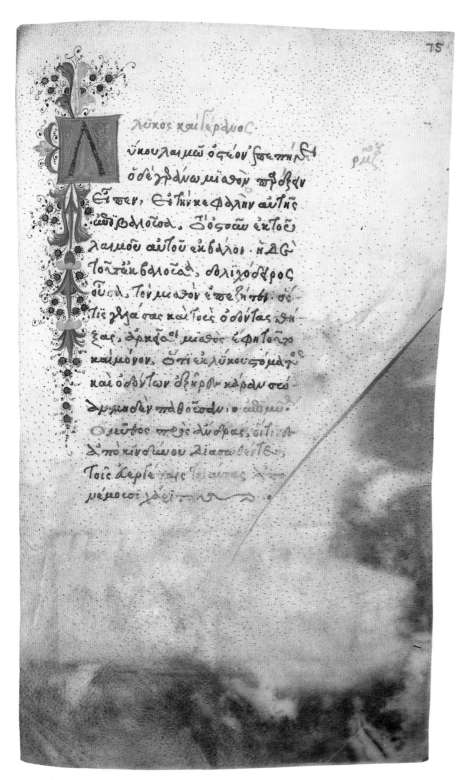

The moral of this fable is: When doing a favor for a wicked man, the good deed itself will have to be your reward.

BIBLIOGRAPHY

Bandini, Angelo Maria. *Catalogus codicum manuscriptorum Bibliothecae Mediceae Laurentianae (accedunt supplementa tria* [1764]. Edited by Enrico Rostagno and Nicola Festa. 2 vols. Leipzig: Zentral-Antiquariaat der Deutschen Demokratischen Republik, 1961.

Bühler, Curt F. *The Fifteenth-Century Book: The Scribes, the Printers, the Decorators*. Philadelphia: University of Pennsylvania Press, 1960.

Fahy, Everett. "Some Early Italian Pictures in the Gambier-Parry Collection." *Burlington Magazine* 109 (March 1967): 128–39.

———. *Some Followers of Domenico Ghirlandajo*. Ph.D. dissertation, Harvard University, 1968. New York and London: Garland Publishing, 1976.

Garzelli, Annarosa, and de la Mare, Albinia. *Miniatura fiorentina del Rinascimento, 1440–1525: Un primo censimento*. Edited by Annarosa Garzelli. 2 vols. Inventari e cataloghi toscani, nos. 18 and 19. Florence: Giunta regionale toscana & La Nuova Italia, 1985.

Kaimowitz, Jeffrey H., and McTigue, Bernard. "Beasts and Landscapes: An Illuminated Florentine Aesop Manuscript of the Fifteenth Century." *Bulletin of Research in the Humanities* 82 (Summer 1979): 139–58.

Küster, Christian Ludwig. "Illustrierte Aesop-Ausgaben des 15. und 16. Jahrhunderts." Ph.D. dissertation, Universität Hamburg, 1970.

Levi d'Ancona, Mirella. *Miniatura e miniatori a Firenze dal XIV al XVI secolo: Documenti per la storia della miniatura*. Florence: Leo S. Olschki, 1962.

Martini, Giuseppe Sergio. *La bottega di un cartolaio fiorentino della seconda metà del Quattrocento: Nuovi contributi biografici intorno a Gherardo e Monte di Giovanni*. Florence: Leo S. Olschki, 1956.

Piccolomini, Enea. "Delle condizioni e delle vicende della Libreria Medicea privata dal 1494 al 1508." *Archivio storico italiano* 19 (1874): 101–29, 254–81; 20 (1874): 51–94; 21 (1875): 102–12, 282–96.

Zeri, Federico. "I frammenti di un celebre Trionfo della Castità." *Quaderni di Emblema*, 1: *Diari di Lavoro*. Bergamo: Emblema Editrice, 1971.

INDEX